DOING ETHNOGRAPHY

Doing Ethnography by Amanda Coffey is the third volume in *The SAGE Qualitative Research Kit*. This book can be used together with the other titles in the *Kit* as a comprehensive guide to the process of doing qualitative research, but is equally valuable on its own as a practical introduction to doing ethnography.

Fully updated and expanded to ten volumes, this second edition of the *Kit* presents the most extensive introduction to the state-of-the-art of qualitative research.

COMPLETE LIST OF TITLES IN *THE SAGE QUALITATIVE RESEARCH KIT*

- *Designing Qualitative Research* **Uwe Flick**
- *Doing Interviews* **Svend Brinkmann and Steinar Kvale**
- *Doing Ethnography* **Amanda Coffey**
- *Doing Focus Groups* **Rosaline Barbour**
- *Using Visual Data in Qualitative Research* **Marcus Banks**
- *Analyzing Qualitative Data* **Graham R. Gibbs**
- *Doing Conversation, Discourse and Document Analysis* **Tim Rapley**
- *Doing Grounded Theory* **Uwe Flick**
- *Doing Triangulation and Mixed Methods* **Uwe Flick**
- *Managing Quality in Qualitative Research* **Uwe Flick**

MEMBERS OF THE EDITORIAL ADVISORY BOARD

DOING ETHNOGRAPHY

AMANDA COFFEY

THE SAGE QUALITATIVE RESEARCH KIT 2ND EDITION

Edited by  Uwe Flick

SSAGE

Los Angeles | London | New Delhi
Singapore | Washington DC | Melbourne

Los Angeles | London | New Delhi
Singapore | Washington DC | Melbourne

SAGE Publications Ltd
1 Oliver's Yard
55 City Road
London EC1Y 1SP

SAGE Publications Inc.
2455 Teller Road
Thousand Oaks, California 91320

SAGE Publications India Pvt Ltd
B 1/I 1 Mohan Cooperative Industrial Area
Mathura Road
New Delhi 110 044

SAGE Publications Asia-Pacific Pte Ltd
3 Church Street
#10-04 Samsung Hub
Singapore 049483

Editor: Mila Steele
Assistant editor: John Nightingale
Production editor: Victoria Nicholas
Copyeditor: Andy Baxter
Proofreader: Rosemary Campbell
Marketing manager: Emma Turner
Cover design: Shaun Mercier
Typeset by C&M Digitals (P) Ltd, Chennai, India
Printed in the UK

Library of Congress Control Number: 2017932322

British Library Cataloguing in Publication data

A catalogue record for this book is available from
the British Library

ISBN 978-1-47391-333-2 (pbk)

At SAGE we take sustainability seriously. Most of our products are printed in the UK using FSC papers and boards.
When we print overseas we ensure sustainable papers are used as measured by the PREPS grading system.
We undertake an annual audit to monitor our sustainability.

For Jake – I promised you a book.

CONTENTS

EDITORIAL INTRODUCTION

UWE FLICK

INTRODUCTION TO *THE SAGE QUALITATIVE RESEARCH KIT*

In recent years, qualitative research has enjoyed a period of unprecedented growth and diversification as it has become an established and respected research approach across a variety of disciplines and contexts. An increasing number of students, teachers and practitioners are facing questions and problems of how to do qualitative research – in general and for their specific individual purposes. To answer these questions, and to address such practical problems on a how-to-do level, is the main purpose of *The SAGE Qualitative Research Kit*.

The books in *The SAGE Qualitative Research Kit* collectively address the core issues that arise when we actually do qualitative research. Each book focuses on key methods (e.g. interviews or focus groups) or materials (e.g. visual data or discourse) that are used for studying the social world in qualitative terms. Moreover, the books in the *Kit* have been written with the needs of many different types of reader in mind. As such, the *Kit* and the individual books will be of use to a wide variety of users:

- *Practitioners* of qualitative research in the social sciences; medical research; marketing research; evaluation; organizational, business and management studies; cognitive science; etc., who face the problem of planning and conducting a specific study using qualitative methods.
- *University teachers* and lecturers in these fields using qualitative methods can use this series as a basis of their teaching.

- *Undergraduate and graduate students* of social sciences, nursing, education, psychology and other fields where qualitative methods are a (main) part of the university training including practical applications (e.g. when writing a thesis).

Each book in *The SAGE Qualitative Research Kit* has been written by distinguished authors with extensive experience in their field and in practice with the methods they write about. When reading the whole series of books from the beginning to the end, you will repeatedly come across some issues which are central to any sort of qualitative research – such as ethics, designing research or assessing quality. However, in each book such issues are addressed from the specific methodological angle of the authors and the approach they describe. Thus you may find different approaches to issues of quality or different suggestions for how to analyze qualitative data in different books, which will combine to present a comprehensive picture of the field as a whole.

WHAT IS QUALITATIVE RESEARCH?

It has become more and more difficult to find a common definition of qualitative research which is accepted by the majority of qualitative research approaches and researchers. Qualitative research is no longer just simply '*not* quantitative research', but has developed an identity (or maybe multiple identities) of its own.

Despite the multiplicity of approaches to qualitative research, some common features of qualitative research can be identified. Qualitative research is intended to approach the world 'out there' (not in specialized research settings such as laboratories) and to understand, describe and sometimes explain social phenomena 'from the inside' in a number of different ways:

- By analyzing experiences of individuals or groups. Experiences can be related to biographical life histories or to (everyday or professional) practices; they may be addressed by analyzing everyday knowledge, accounts and stories.
- By analyzing interactions and communications in the making. This can be based on observing or recording practices of interacting and communicating and analyzing this material.
- By analyzing documents (texts, images, film or music) or similar traces of experiences or interactions.

Common to such approaches is that they seek to unpick how people construct the world around them, what they are doing or what is happening to them in terms that are meaningful and that offer rich insight. Interactions and documents are seen as ways of constituting social processes and artefacts collaboratively (or conflictingly). All of these approaches represent ways of meaning, which can be reconstructed and analyzed with different qualitative methods that allow the researcher to develop (more or less generalizable) models, typologies, theories as ways of describing and explaining social (or psychological) issues.

HOW DO WE CONDUCT QUALITATIVE RESEARCH?

Can we identify common ways of doing qualitative research if we take into account that there are different theoretical, epistemological and methodological approaches to qualitative research and that the issues that are studied are very diverse as well? We can at least identify some common features of how qualitative research is done.

- Qualitative researchers are interested in accessing experiences, interactions and documents in their natural context and in a way that gives room to the particularities of them and the materials in which they are studied.
- Qualitative research refrains from setting up a well-defined concept of what is studied and from formulating hypotheses in the beginning in order to test them. Rather, concepts (or hypotheses, if they are used) are developed and refined in the process of research.
- Qualitative research starts from the idea that methods and theories should be appropriate to what is studied. If the existing methods do not fit with a concrete issue or field, they are adapted or new methods or approaches are developed.
- Researchers themselves are an important part of the research process, either in terms of their own personal presence as researchers, or in terms of their experiences in the field and with the reflexivity they bring to the role – as are members of the field under study.
- Qualitative research takes context and cases seriously for understanding an issue under study. A lot of qualitative research is based on case studies or a series of case studies, and often the case (its history and complexity) is an important context for understanding what is studied.
- A major part of qualitative research is based on texts and writing – from field notes and transcripts to descriptions and interpretations and finally to the presentation of the findings and of the research as a whole. Therefore, issues of transforming complex social situations (or other materials such as images) into texts – issues of transcribing and writing in general – are major concerns of qualitative research.

- If methods are supposed to be adequate to what is under study, approaches to defining and assessing the quality of qualitative research (still) have to be discussed in specific ways that are appropriate for qualitative research and even for specific approaches in qualitative research.

SCOPE OF *THE SAGE QUALITATIVE RESEARCH KIT*

Designing Qualitative Research (Uwe Flick) gives a brief introduction to qualitative research from the point of view of how to plan and design a concrete study using qualitative research in one way or another. It is intended to outline a framework for the other books in *The SAGE Qualitative Research Kit* by focusing on how-to-do problems and on how to solve such problems in the research process. The book addresses issues of constructing a research design in qualitative research; it outlines stumbling blocks in making a research project work and discusses practical problems such as resources in qualitative research but also more methodological issues like quality of qualitative research and also ethics. This framework is filled out in more detail in the other books in the *Kit*.

Three books are devoted to collecting or producing data in qualitative research. They take up the issues briefly outlined in the first book and approach them in a much more detailed and focused way for the specific method. First, *Doing Interviews* (Svend Brinkmann and Steinar Kvale) addresses the theoretical, epistemological, ethical and practical issues of interviewing people about specific issues or their life history. *Doing Ethnography* (Amanda Coffey) focuses on the second major approach to collecting and producing qualitative data. Here again practical issues (like selecting sites, methods of collecting data in ethnography, special problems of analyzing them) are discussed in the context of more general issues (ethics, representations, quality and adequacy of ethnography as an approach). In *Doing Focus Groups* (Rosaline Barbour) the third of the most important qualitative methods of producing data is presented. Here again we find a strong focus on how-to-do issues of sampling, designing and analyzing the data and on how to produce them in focus groups.

Three further volumes are devoted to analyzing specific types of qualitative data. *Using Visual Data in Qualitative Research* (Marcus Banks) extends the focus to the third type of qualitative data (beyond verbal data coming from interviews and focus groups and observational data). The use of visual data has not only become a major trend in social research in general, but confronts researchers with new practical problems in using them and analyzing them and produces new ethical issues. In *Analyzing Qualitative Data* (Graham R. Gibbs), several practical approaches and issues of making sense of any sort of qualitative data are addressed. Special attention is paid to practices of coding, of comparing and of using computer-assisted qualitative data analysis. Here, the focus is on verbal data, like interviews, focus groups or biographies. *Doing Conversation, Discourse and Document Analysis* (Tim Rapley) extends this focus to different types of data, relevant for analyzing discourses. Here, the focus is on existing material (like documents) and on recording everyday conversations and on finding traces of discourses. Practical issues such as generating an archive, transcribing video materials and how to analyze discourses with such types of data are discussed.

Three final volumes go beyond specific forms of data or single methods and take a broader approach. *Doing Grounded Theory* (Uwe Flick) focuses on an integrated research programme in qualitative research. *Doing Triangulation and Mixed Methods* (Uwe Flick) addresses combinations of several approaches in qualitative research or with quantitative methods. *Managing Quality in Qualitative Research* (Uwe Flick) takes up the issue of quality in qualitative research, which has been briefly addressed in specific contexts in other books in the *Kit*, in a more general way. Here, quality is looked at from the angle of using or reformulating existing criteria, or defining new criteria, for qualitative research. This book examines the ongoing debates about what should count as defining 'quality' and validity in qualitative methodologies and examines the many strategies for promoting and managing quality in qualitative research.

Before I go on to outline the focus of this book and its role in the *Kit*, I would like to thank some people at SAGE who were important in making this *Kit* happen. Michael Carmichael suggested this project to me some time ago and was very helpful with his suggestions in the beginning. Patrick Brindle, Katie Metzler and Mila Steele took over and continued this support, as did Victoria Nicholas and John Nightingale in making books out of the manuscripts we provided.

ABOUT THIS BOOK

UWE FLICK

In the early as well as in the more recent development of qualitative research, ethnography has played a major role. Much of what we know about field relations, about openness and directedness towards a field and its members is known from research in ethnography. Although ethnography is closely linked to the method of **participant observation**, and was based on it or maybe has replaced it more recently, ethnography always included a variety of methods of data collection. Quite often we find combinations of observation, participation, more or less formal interviewing and the use of documents and other traces of events in ethnography. At the same time, not every relevant issue is accessible for ethnography, participation and observation. Sampling in this context is less focused on people to select for the research than on selecting fields or institutions, or more generally, sites for observation. Towards the end of the twentieth century, methodological discussions in ethnography more and more shifted from issues of data collection and finding a role in the field to questions of writing about and reporting from the field, the research and the experiences in it. Analyzing ethnographic data is often oriented towards searching for patterns of behaviours, interactions and practices.

In this book such key topics of doing ethnography are unfolded in some detail. Whereas the other books are more focused on verbal data, like interviews (Brinkmann and Kvale, 2018) or focus groups (Barbour, 2018), or concentrate on analyzing conversations (Rapley, 2018) or images (Banks, 2018), *Doing Ethnography* brings the pragmatics of field research into the scope of *The SAGE Qualitative Research Kit*. At the same time, it can be complemented by more detailed analysis of using these sources (from interviews to visual data) in the more general context of ethnography. The books on analyzing data (Gibbs, 2018), designs and quality in qualitative research (Flick, 2018a, 2018b) triangulation (Flick, 2018c) and grounded theory (Flick, 2018d) add some extra context to what is outlined here in some detail. Together these books and this one allow us to decide when to use ethnography and observation and provide a methodological and theoretical basis for using this strategy in the field. The exemplary studies repeatedly used for illustration in this book are helpful for seeing ethnography not so much as a method but more as a strategy, and when it is appropriate to issues and fields under study.

ACKNOWLEDGEMENTS

I am very grateful to Uwe Flick for the invitation to write this volume and to contribute to *The SAGE Qualitative Research Kit*. I would like to particularly acknowledge his patience and support during the writing process. I would like to thank colleagues in the School of Social Sciences at Cardiff University for their continuing collegiality and support. Much love and thanks to Julian Pitt for keeping heart and home together, and to my wonderful children Jake and Thomas, just for being you.

CHAPTER ONE

INTRODUCTION

THE FOUNDATIONS OF ETHNOGRAPHY

CONTENTS

After reading this chapter, you will:

- have a working definition of the term 'ethnography';
- be able to differentiate between ethnography as a description of a research method and as a research product;
- have an appreciation of the historical context of ethnography;
- know about some of the key theoretical and disciplinary influences on the development of ethnography; and
- understand some of the key principles and practices that underpin ethnographic work.

WHAT IS ETHNOGRAPHY?

Ethnography is a term used within the social sciences and humanities to describe and define a social research method, or more accurately a set of methods for understanding and making sense of cultural and social worlds. In literal translation ethnography means the writing ('graphy') of people ('ethno'). Ethnography encompasses a range of data collection techniques for gathering qualitative information about a setting, and usually incorporates some kind of researcher participation within the daily life of the setting. Data collection in ethnographic research actually draws on many of the skills and methods social actors routinely use to navigate their own daily lives – for example, using techniques such as observation, listening, asking questions, gathering documents and recording information. In ethnography such routine and everyday practices are used, in systematic and reflective ways, in order to generate analyses and understanding.

Ethnographic methods are part of a broad umbrella of qualitative research approaches for documenting and understanding social and cultural life. Indeed, the terms 'ethnography' and 'qualitative research' are often used interchangeably. Moreover, ethnography is often viewed as a foundation stone of contemporary, and increasingly varied, qualitative research practices. Qualitative research in general, encompassing and drawing on ethnographic methods, has become increasingly utilized across many areas of social science, humanities and cognate fields including social anthropology, sociology, criminology, religious studies, health studies and education.

Ethnography is, then, a term used to describe a set of methods for collecting qualitative information, in order to develop and inform our understandings of everyday lives and cultures. Ethnography is also a term that is used to describe the product of, or outcome from, ethnographic research. The production or writing of ethnography is a craft skill, enabling the researcher (as author) to draw together both diverse materials and interpretation in ways that tell of a place and people. 'Ethnographies' in this sense of the term, are crafted reports of research, utilizing qualitative data and analysis in order to provide rich descriptions of the social setting being studied. Such reportage is usually in the form of a written text, which provides narration, but can also include other kinds of data display – photographs, moving images, poetry, documents, performance pieces and artefacts – in order to 'write' of and re-present the setting.

A BRIEF HISTORY OF ETHNOGRAPHY

The ethnographic approach to studying people in their social and cultural context has a long history, most readily traced back to the work of social and cultural anthropology of the late nineteenth and early twentieth centuries; where anthropological scholars became concerned with studying and understanding 'other' societies through close, lived engagement. For example, scholars in the first quarter of the twentieth century, among them the Polish anthropologist Bronislaw Malinowski and the English social anthropologist Alfred Radcliffe-Brown, developed the idea of immersion and engagement in a setting in order to understand the human condition. Reflecting their time, such scholars drew on particular understandings and experiences of colonial life, undertaking anthropological **fieldwork**, often for extended periods of time, in places such as Africa and the Pacific Islands, in order to examine the ways in which 'other' societies functioned and were structured. The approach they took was, at the time in question, a significant departure in relation to researching traditional cultures, representing a move away from an evolutionary approach to societal development, towards a more detailed exploration of the everyday, practical accomplishment of social life through institutions and relationships. With the benefit of hindsight, it is clear that colonial influences had significant impact on the ways in which these 'traditional' societies operated, and indeed came to be understood by anthropological inquiry. That is, there is a persuasive argument that the anthropological gaze served to compound some of the very impact of colonial rule; extended anthropological field trips, often including long periods of residence, arguably did much to perpetuate the colonial 'othering' of particular cultures and people. A specific example of this is Malinowski's ethnographies of the Trobriand Islands in the Pacific Ocean, of which one of the most cited works was titled *The Sexual Life of Savages in North-Western Melanesia* (1929); such a title is almost unthinkable in contemporary postcolonial times.

In North America, the anthropological interest at the turn of the twentieth century was somewhat closer to home. Rather than focusing on distant 'other' cultures and societies, North American scholars developed a social–cultural anthropological approach to studying (and in some ways reconstructing) the cultural life of 'native' American peoples. One such researcher, Franz Boas, a German physicist turned US anthropologist, was particularly influential in developing the anthropological interest in culture and language. Dismissive of what were then evolutionary approaches to the study of culture (and indeed also of biological–scientific racism), Boas articulated more nuanced understandings of difference between societies or social groups as a result of social learning – that is, as differences of culture rather than of biology. In so doing, Boas developed the important anthropological concept of **cultural relativism** – which might usefully be described as both an imperative and a willingness to suspend one's own cultural assumptions in order to understand social structures, belief systems and practices from *within* a culture. Cultural relativism provided a framework for studying and seeking to understand a culture on and in its own terms through its own cultural frame of reference. Boas helped to shape cultural anthropology in the USA and across the world, with many of his students, such as Margaret Mead and Ruth Benedict, going on to influence the discipline over the course of the twentieth century.

While there were differences in the development of the social and cultural anthropological traditions across both sides of the Atlantic, in relation to both choice of sites for study and the lens through which societies were seen, there were also considerable similarities of practice. These early pioneers of what came to be identified as ethnography advocated a prolonged engagement with the society or culture to be studied, with immersion of the researcher held up as a standard to which ethnographers should aspire. That is, there was recognition of fieldwork in the setting as a means to understanding the everyday practices in and of that setting. Ethnographic research does not have to involve extended engagement, perhaps over several months or years, or full participation and immersion on the part of the researcher within the culture. However, the very idea of understanding a setting from the point of view of those engaged in that setting, and doing so through on the ground engagement in and with that setting, remains a powerful underpinning of contemporary ethnographic approaches.

The School of Sociology at the University of Chicago is often credited with bringing ethnography to wider sociological attention, drawing on anthropological sensibilities in more mundane research settings. Founded in 1892, the Chicago

School was the first dedicated university department of sociology, and is responsible for helping to shape the social sciences, both empirically and methodologically. With an emphasis on urban sociology, The Chicago School of the 1920s and 1930s theorized about the city, drawing on ethnographic research of Chicago and its environs. Chicago scholars encouraged their students to get first-hand experience of social life in different parts of the city. To do so they adapted the idea of engaged fieldwork, including participant observation, to study the contemporary urban cityscape. The journalist Robert Park, alongside Ernest Burgess and W.I. Thomas, was a key figure in the development of the Chicago School, bringing with him an early interpretation of investigative journalism, relying on ethnographic methods of sorts – listening, experiencing, asking questions and observing social life first-hand. This brought anthropological ethnographic methods 'home', using participant observation to study familiar and everyday settings on the doorstep, as opposed to the study of the 'exotic' or 'different' that had been favoured by early social and cultural anthropologists.

Park and his colleagues transformed the study of the city, through close and varied empirical and ethnographic inquiry. Following the Second World War, this influence endured, with students learning about and practising interpretative sociology and ethnographic methods with scholars such as Everett Hughes and Herbert Blumer. This 'second' Chicago School was a key influence in shaping the development of post-war American sociology, and indeed the discipline more generally (Fine, 1995). The Chicago School approach is credited with influencing the ways in which social institutions are studied and understood by sociologists; this influence has been wide reaching, including in fields such as health care and education, as well as organizational studies more generally. The way was also paved for the wider adoption of qualitative research methods in the medium term, grounded in and emergent from ethnography. This influence though was not just in relation to methods of inquiry, but also relatedly to sociological theory and methodology. The Chicago School was pivotal in the development of the theoretical perspective and frameworks of **symbolic interactionism**. Drawing on the philosophical work of George Herbert Mead, symbolic interactionism focused on shared meanings that are generated and maintained through social interaction. While not exclusively so, symbolic interactionism has been particularly associated with ethnography and qualitative research methods, with its emphasis on meaning and process, and 'where acts, objects and people have evolving and intertwined local identities that may not be revealed at the outset or to an outsider' (Rock, 2001, p. 29). In the next section the theoretical and methodological frames of and for ethnography are further explored.

THE METHODOLOGICAL CONTEXTS OF ETHNOGRAPHY

Ethnographic research is now practised across a wide range of disciplines, and as such it draws on a rich palette of theoretical and methodological frameworks. It is important to note that ethnography lends itself to and is influenced by a variety of theoretical positions. Ethnography is not reduced to a single approach to theorizing about the social world. Indeed ethnography has been adopted and shaped by a range of methodological approaches to the making sense of social life. It is generally understood that ethnography sits at the inductive end of the theoretical spectrum, and that a value of ethnography is its capacity to enable study of social worlds in their 'natural' state – inductively through close and detailed attention. Early adopters of anthropological ethnography began with a specific setting, culture or community at hand – and set out to learn about and understand that setting through close study and participative engagement. They did not start, at least explicitly, from the position of a hypothesis to be tested or a theory to prove or improve. However, early ethnographic practitioners were increasingly influenced by a view of the social world that is orderly and functional, and by an understanding that society is achieved by organization and through social institutions. This functionalist–structural perspective included a focus on the role of social institutions in supporting the everyday functioning of society (and indeed in turn led to a particular preoccupation with the role of the family and kinship as a particular, and presumed universal, social institution). A focus on structure and function led to the pursuit of ethnography as an empirical project, where social action, behaviour and belief are revealed as social 'facts' to be gathered – 'objectively' and untainted by researchers, who are but neutral observers. Inherent within this model is a rather uncritical adoption of a naturalistic perspective. That is, a view that social worlds can and should be studied in their natural states, with the main aim being to describe what is actually and naturally happening. Following this through to a natural conclusion, if we are to understand what it is we are describing then we need an approach that provides access to behaviour and the patterning of that behaviour. Thus prolonged engagement provides the opportunity to observe and to learn, coming to understand the ordering and functioning of the social world in much the same way as the social actors themselves.

Symbolic interactionism, influenced by the Chicago School of Sociology, focuses less on institutions and the identification of patterning, and much more on the ways in which human actions are imbued with social meanings which are made and revealed through social interaction. Thus people, as social actors, are active and interactive agents in social worlds where there is continual interpretation, revision and reshaping. This is a more dynamic and moving view of social life, and one which brings with it an assumption of the self as socially constructed, and 'made' through action and interaction. In terms of ethnography, symbolic interactionism brought to the fore a focus on meanings and symbols; less a focus on objects and behaviours than on how they are and come to be imbued with social and symbolic meaning. There is also an interest in how social actors learn and interpret these meanings in and through their everyday practice. These meanings are uncovered through an exploration of the symbols in which meanings are encoded, and shared in the course of interaction. Interactionist ethnography does not 'presume too much in advance' (Rock, 2001, p. 29); rather, through ethnographic fieldwork researchers can seek to identify symbols and meanings in order to gain understandings of how social actors act in and make sense of social worlds. Such ethnographic work assumes an immersion in the social world in order to make sense of that world from the perspective of the actors themselves. Interactionism is one of the major perspectives or set of perspectives within sociology. There are a variety of versions of interactionism; for ethnography the interactionism associated with Erving Goffman (1959, 1963, 1967, 1969) has been particularly influential. Goffman himself did not explicitly identify himself as an interactionist (Fine and Manning, 2003). However, his work on the purposive construction of the self through active impression management – the presentation of self – highlights the ways in which people describe their actions and how they 'perform' the self. Goffman likened this to performance and drama; this dramaturgical approach is concerned with how social actors purposively act in different situations and how they make sense of those actions in terms of meanings. Performativity remains a key concept in contemporary ethnography.

The influence of symbolic interactionism on ethnography is most obvious in relation to the ways in which we describe ethnography itself as an interactional process. We 'do' ethnography; doing ethnography is an act in itself – reliant upon and constructed through interactions between the ethnographer, the field of study and social actors with/in the field. There is here a focus on participation – with the researcher being a participant in and within the setting in order to uncover and make sense of meanings. There has been considerable debate on the extent to which ethnographers can and should participate in the field of study (Adler and Adler, 1994). This is often expressed as a continuum from 'complete participant' on the one side through to 'complete observer' on the other (see Chapter 5 for a longer discussion of the role of the researcher in ethnography). For our purposes here it is worth noting that interactionism makes visible the importance and impact of researcher engagement in the field and the significance of interaction for the ethnographic process itself.

Ethnography has also been influenced by, and in turn has influenced, the theoretical work of **ethnomethodology** (Pollner and Emerson, 2001). Ethnomethodologists are particularly concerned with the understanding of social life at the micro-level and through uncovering meaning in the close and detailed study of interaction. Ethnographic approaches are also used in order to pay close attention to social life at this micro-level. Both ethnomethodology and ethnography are situated within the interpretive social sciences, and are concerned with understanding the life worlds of social actors in the context of their setting. While the two perspectives have had different followers and have not always been aligned, they have nonetheless 'grown older together ... where once clearer boundaries have become blurred' (Pollner and Emerson, 2001, p. 118). Ethnomethodology, like ethnography, has had a wide disciplinary appeal, including from within sociology and discursive psychology, and has been particularly concerned with the ways in which reality and social order are constructed and maintained through interaction. Ethnomethodologists have a particular interest in language – including spoken words and conversations, but also sounds, gestures and body language. There is an interest in the sequencing of language, alongside spatial and temporal contexts; and thus in how social actors work *together* to construct and maintain social order, and at times to change that order in nuanced and subtle ways. So, from an ethnographic perspective, there is a resonance and shift from a preoccupation with culture or society itself towards the techniques through which interactional realities are maintained; how people use and identify social cues, what is said and left unsaid, how reciprocal relations are shaped and reinforced, and what methods people use used to persuade each other of society and the shared sense of order. Ethnomethodologists have used and developed ethnographical approaches in order to collect what might be identified as naturally occurring interactional data, such as conversations and other language encounters (Silverman, 2011). The analysis of these encounters has helped to uncover techniques through which social actors develop and perform shared understandings, persuading each other of the society of which they are parts. There has been considerable debate about ongoing similarities and differences between ethnomethodology and ethnography (Atkinson, 1988), within a context of recognition that dialogue between the two is ethnographically valuable, expanding the appreciation of 'the depth, limits and complexity of its own practices and those of the persons or groups comprising its substantive focus' (Pollner and Emerson, 2001, p. 131).

FEMINIST ETHNOGRAPHY

Like qualitative research more generally, ethnography has also been shaped by, and has helped to define feminist scholarship and research practice. The dialogue between feminism and ethnography can be situated within feminist critiques of social science and social research more generally. There have been nuanced understandings of the ways in which the ideologies of gender have structured the social relations of research, alongside considerable philosophical debate about the gendered nature of knowledge (Harding, 1987; Ramazanoglu and Holland, 2002). Feminist theorists have critiqued some of the established assumptions that have underpinned social scientific inquiry, calling into question underlying perceived dichotomies – such as objectivity/subjectivity and rationality/emotionality – as well as repositioning and restating knowledge as grounded, local, partial and temporally situated. Such insights have led to a feminist research agenda and to a recasting of feminist social research – where the conditions of knowledge production are critically acknowledged and accounted for, where issues of power are recognized in the research process and in relation to research production, and where **epistemology** and ontology are central (Letherby, 2003). As Stanley has eloquently described, 'feminism is not merely a perspective, a way of seeing; nor even this plus an epistemology, a way of knowing; it is also an ontology, a way of being in the world' (1990, p. 14).

It is now widely accepted that feminist research methods can incorporate a wide variety of approaches, both quantitative and qualitative; as Letherby (2003) notes, feminists can count as well as quote. It is certainly not the case that some methods are more inherently feminist than others, and feminist scholars have used a variety of approaches to empirical work and knowledge creation. Within that general context, feminist researchers have used and developed ethnographic approaches to reveal women's standpoints (Farrell, 1992; Langellier and Hall, 1989) and have debated the representation of feminist ethnography in and through the production of texts (Behar and Gordon, 1995; Clough, 1992). Feminist anthropologists, for example, have engaged in an epistemological and methodological project towards establishing a distinctive feminist ethnography (see Jennaway, 1990; Schrock, 2013; Walter, 1995). Abu-Lughod (1990) posed the question as to whether there can be a feminist ethnography, and if so what that might look like. This included a focus on the ways in which feminist ethnography might enable exploration of the relationship between feminism and **reflexivity**, troubling the distinction between objectivity and subjectivity, and considering the power in and of writing. Abu-Lughod spoke of an 'unsettling of the boundaries that have been central to its identity as a discipline of the self-studying other' (1990, p. 26). Jennaway similarly argued that postmodern discourses in ethnography borrowed from and emerged out of feminist preoccupations and articulations, including a move towards egalitarian relations of textual production, more dialogic and collaborative approaches and a 'move away from systems of representation which objectify and silence the ethnographic other' (1990, p. 171). Reflecting on the methodological imperatives of feminist ethnography in contemporary times, Schrock (2013) identifies the importance of representation (both its benefits and detriments) and ethical responsibility towards the communities where researchers work and study.

POSTMODERNISM

The postmodern turn in social science provides a methodological backdrop for contemporary ethnography, influencing the methodology and practice in a number of ways (Fontana and McGinnis, 2003). In simple terms, **postmodernism** represented a rejection of an objective reality and science, in favour of a more complex, nuanced, multi-layered understanding of the social world. Postmodernism, which can be taken as a movement influenced by and influencing a variety of theoretical and methodological approaches – including feminism but also postcolonialism, critical theory, critical race theory and queer theory among others – recognizes and celebrates a diversity of perspectives. Postmodern approaches to understanding and theorizing value the importance of the understanding of context for making sense of behaviours and meanings. Moreover, postmodern approaches raise important questions about power and authority in social research and the production of knowledge. There comes with postmodernism a critical questioning of hegemony and an inherent belief in providing opportunities to 'give voice'. There is also the recognition that social worlds are multiple, layered and polyvocal, and that there are many voices to be heard; also that social worlds are dialogic, constructed by social actors who bring with them different histories, biographies and experiences. Hence there is a fundamental articulation of social worlds as socially constructed and represented, where the self gets positioned and repositioned within and through social and cultural contexts. Thus, in relation to postmodern ethnography, there is a focus on exploring and recognizing the contexts through which social worlds are constructed and lives lived, as well as on providing more nuanced vehicles for documenting social worlds and taking into account the multiple voices that are present and must be heard. Postmodern approaches to ethnography have placed a particular emphasis on the products of ethnography and on finding alternative ways of representing and reporting social data, in order to better give voice to, and to work with rather than on, social actors in research settings. In so doing, postmodern ethnographers have also posed questions about power and authority in our research encounters, as well as about the authoritative text of the scholarly ethnographic monograph.

PRINCIPLES AND PRACTICES

There are a diversity of perspectives and theoretical positions from which ethnography has been derived and developed. Despite this, and while recognizing that ethnography can incorporate a variety of methods for data collection, analysis and representation, there are a number of principles and practices which most ethnographers would endorse. Such principles and practices are partly to do with the ways in which ethnographic researchers go about conceptualizing problems, but also focus on the underlying theoretical and methodological frameworks which guide the research endeavour.

The first of these ethnographic principles is to understand the importance of context in seeking to make sense of a culture or social setting. Social actors, events, actions and interactions must be seen and understood in relation to the cultural context in which they are situated. This includes paying attention to the local circumstances, as well as to the historical, spatial, temporal and organizational frames of a setting and of social lives lived of and within that setting. This, then, is a recognition that accounts of settings have to be contextualized in relation to the totality of that setting. This commitment means not making premature assumptions about what or who is important and striving to develop a better understanding of the context in which and through which things are done and things are said. This broader view means that the significance of particular people, actions, events and interactions may only retrospectively become clear. This also means being absolutely apparent that, as social researchers or ethnographers, we cannot ever produce a complete or exhaustive account or analysis of a setting. Rather, by appreciating the complexity of a setting, ethnographers are then able to be selective in their observations and analysis in order to produce a coherent account. Such accounts are always partial and should be acknowledged as such. This commitment to holism – to situating the particular within the broader context while also recognizing that it is rarely or indeed ever possible to gain a complete picture – is central to the ethnographic enterprise.

Attention to process is also a badge of ethnographic research. Process in the ethnographic context can mean two different but related things. The first, drawing on the interactionist tradition, emphasizes that social life is itself fluid and moving, a process rather than a fixed and bounded entity. Thus social life is emergent out of processes of action and interaction. Ethnographers are interested in how interactional processes are enacted and understood in order to give order and meaning to social life. Ethnographers explore patterns, structures and routines through which interaction provides meaning. The second ethnographic commitment to process is with the research process itself, always paying close and reflexive attention to the ways in which research takes place and to the approaches through which the researcher accesses the site of study, builds rapport and trust, and shapes the focus and outcomes of the research.

Most ethnographic research is also usually 'field' based, that is undertaken in situ – with/in the research settings and conducted first-hand, by the researchers themselves. This is a commitment again to context, but also to participant experience. The primary instrument of data collection in ethnography is the researcher, who is in various ways engaged in observing, listening, asking, interacting and recording. This also assumes a commitment on behalf of the researcher to the research setting and the people, and usually some kind of prolonged and/or deep engagement. This can be really, properly long-term engagement, sometimes over several years or decades. But it can also mean a matter of weeks or series of hours. There is something here about the quality of the engagement rather than a preoccupation with time spent.

Undertaking ethnographic research also recognizes the dialogic and interactional nature of social life. Ethnographers are committed to identifying and recording the perspectives and understandings of social actors. There is an awareness that social realities are complex and multiple, and may be competing; and that there may be a range of perspectives and many voices. There is an acknowledgement and acceptance that social actors are themselves knowledgeable and skilful incumbents of their own social and cultural worlds. They are the experts here, and the role of the researcher is to recognize and attempt to capture those highly developed sets of knowledges and skills.

The ethnographic approach to research also seeks to make sense of both talking and doing. Alongside a focus on action and activity within a social setting, is an understanding that social actors account for their actions, and in ways that might differ from what actually happens. There is not a superficial concern here with how people might do one thing and say another. Nor are we seeking out inconsistencies between what people do and what they say they do. Rather, taking accounts seriously in ethnographic work provides a way of investigating and understanding both how people make sense of what they do and how they do the things they do. Moreover, by focusing on talking and doing ethnographers are able to explore both action and meaning.

Finally, ethnography is not only a way of seeing or hearing, but also a way of telling. Ethnography includes a commitment and an imperative to re-present and represent social life. Writing – producing the 'ethnography' – is a central part of the ethnographic endeavour, not something that simply happens after the research event. Writing is part of the research process and requires the same reflexive attention as other aspects of the research act. Conventionally, the 'ethnography' has been conceptualized as a scholarly narrative monograph, in which and through which the ethnographer tells the story of the research setting, usually through literary conventions of narrative prose. However, there are a range of ways in which ethnographers can represent the field and tell the story of the research setting. The principle can thus be extended to a broader range of ethnographic production, whereby ethnographers are concerned to provide representational and reflexive accounts of their research, drawing on a range of conventions and genres, which may include literature, art, film and performance.

KEY POINTS

- Ethnography is concerned with understanding social worlds through researcher engagement and participation.
- Ethnography is a term that is used to describe a research process and a research product.
- Modern ethnography emerged out of social and cultural anthropological practice of the late nineteenth and early twentieth centuries; used in order to study small 'traditional' societies.
- Ethnographic methods are now used by researchers from across a broad spectrum of disciplines and fields of study, to investigate a wide range of settings.
- Ethnography has been influenced by and has influenced a range of theoretical and methodological perspectives, including feminism, ethnomethodology, social interactionism and postmodernism.
- Key principles of ethnographic research practice include:

  o understanding the importance of context in studying social settings and social lives;
  o attention to process in social life and in research;
  o researcher engagement and participation in the research setting;
  o recognizing the dialogic and interactional nature of social life;
  o a commitment to writing and representation.

FURTHER READING

Atkinson, P. and Hammersley, M. (2007) *Ethnography: Principles in Practice*, 3rd ed. London: Routledge.
Gobo, G. (2008) *Doing Ethnography*. London: Sage.
O'Reilly, K. (2008) *Key Concepts in Ethnography*. London: Sage.

CHAPTER TWO

ETHNOGRAPHY AND RESEARCH DESIGN

CONTENTS

OBJECTIVES

After reading this chapter, you will:

- have an understanding of the kinds of research topics, problems and settings that might be particularly well suited to an ethnographic approach;
- be able to identify some of the methods available for data generation in ethnographic research; and
- have an appreciation of the ethnographic research process, including the relationship between data collection and data analysis.

DESIGNING AN ETHNOGRAPHIC PROJECT

Planning an ethnographic research project is both exciting and challenging, precisely because of the lack of a tightly bounded or formulaic approach to research design. Ethnography relies on a close and detailed engagement with a setting, community or group of social actors, and is predicated on an understanding that we learn 'about' by being 'with/in'. Thus, it follows, that an important aspect of an ethnographic project is the 'getting on with it' – involvement in the setting quickly and in ways that promote engagement and understanding. This might include observing, listening, asking questions, and indeed gathering any and all information you can lay your hands on – including documents, photographs and other materials from and about a setting. Such an immediate approach to ethnographic fieldwork is, to an extent at least, encouraged and supported by and through the theoretical foundations on which ethnographic research sits – with a focus on an inductive approach to theory building; generating ideas and analyses 'bottom up', from the ground and with an open mind. How better to pursue this than by moving forward quickly with fieldwork? And there is merit in such a timely approach, certainly with not delaying early data collection unnecessarily in favour of lengthy desk-based preparation time. Ethnographic research is often best served by early engagement and dialogue with the field of study. However, it is a mistake to think that there is an absence of preparedness or research design in ethnography. Like in all social scientific research, in ethnographic study there are choices to be made, issues of research design (Flick, 2018a) to address and to decide upon with thoughtfulness and care. While it is important not to predetermine the outcomes or experiences of fieldwork, or be overly prescriptive (we should always be prepared to be surprised and to be flexible in our approach), preparedness is still key to a successful ethnographic project.

There are a number of aspects of ethnographic research design that require careful consideration and at least a degree of planning. These include defining an initial research 'problem', question or topic for exploration and investigation, and identifying data collection and analytical strategies for the ways in which those ideas will be taken forward, developed and refined. The research setting and/or participants must also be identified, and this in itself might well involve preliminary research and fieldwork. There are real choices for the ethnographer in relation to generating data, managing data and undertaking analyses; not least because ethnography speaks to and includes a variety of approaches. Equally there are a range of ways in which ethnographic research can be written about, represented and reported. Ethnographic research, with its repertoire of methods, is also particularly well suited to be used in combination with other complementary approaches, thus prompting further issues for thoughtful research design. If and when ethnography is used in combination, good design is required to ensure that the final project benefits from the sum of the parts.

IDENTIFYING SUITABLE TOPICS AND PROBLEMS

Ethnography is best suited to topics of exploration and discovery, rather than to questions of causality or narrow policy evaluation. Ethnographic research provides mechanisms for gaining understanding or exploring meaning as opposed to testing variables or identifying causes. Thus topics and questions that are suitable for ethnographic treatment are those which address process and practice – for example, how do things happen in the ways that they do? How are everyday activities organized? How do people in settings perceive and understand their daily work and lives? Questions such as these might be useful starting points for helping to identify a topic for exploration. Such questions are concerned with an intellectual curiosity for wanting to gain layered understandings of settings, communities, groups and cultures. They might also be accompanied by questions about or concerns with what matters within such settings – for example, what do people regard as important to them in their daily lives or work? What strategies are employed by people in order to get through or make sense of their experiences? What categories and devices are used by people to order, make sense of and account for actions and events? There is a long and distinguished tradition of **institutional ethnography** – of ethnographies of organizations for which such questions are particularly well suited. But ethnographic research does not need to be restricted to institutional settings, important and interesting though they are or might be. So alongside topics and questions which might enable detailed explorations of institutions such as schools, hospitals, business settings and prisons, the same curiosity in relation to 'what' and 'how' can be equally applicable to taxi drivers, family life, competitive swimmers, youth gangs or welfare activists. A key point here is that ethnographic research is an appropriate choice where questions focus on exploration and discovery, as well as on understanding settings from the perspectives of those who inhabit such spaces. Or to turn that around, ethnographic research can in and of itself be used to identify and define a research 'problem'; that is, a focus of further exploration to aid understanding and sense making. Ethnographic research is also well suited to understanding and documenting process. This recognizes that social settings are dynamic and shifting spaces, with fluid boundaries and multiple perspectives that are brought to bear. There is a perception that ethnography is best suited to studying 'naturally occurring' settings, events and happenings – that are simply 'there' to be observed and understood. It is true that ethnography does not set out to 'create' artificial laboratory conditions through which to understand lives and cultures; however, there is a recognition that daily lives and settings are not in themselves particularly 'naturally occurring', but rather shaped and maintained through social and cultural boundaries and interactions.

Research questions help to formulate a structure through which we can seek to make sense of processes, practices, organizations, settings and lives in ethnographic research. In a spirit of discovery such questions should be open rather than closed, attendant to the possibilities rather than concerned with narrow and definitive answers. Ethnographic research does not and should not start with a lack of ideas or questions; we do not enter a setting with an empty mind, but rather an open mind. Openness in ethnographic research gives permission for refinement, for refreshing the topics to be examined and the problems to be explored. A 'foreshadowed problem', after Malinowski (1922) is a helpful concept here. A foreshadowed problem is not a problem in the sense of a problem to be resolved or solved. Rather it is a way of describing a 'research problem' – a topic to be explored or investigated or better understood. Foreshadowed problems can be identified through a range of sources – for example, from a personal interest in a setting or phenomenon, from theoretical work or comparative projects, from something that just appears interesting or unusual or unexplained, or from a chance encounter or opportune experience. Foreshadowed problems help us to both focus and to develop a set of open, reflective areas for initial exploration – important in designing an ethnographic project. Having a focus, with open and reflexive lines of inquiry to guide initial observation, listening and questioning will lead to a purposive and meaningful project. Foreshadowed problems can be used to develop guiding questions for the ethnographer to explore; they must also be identified in such a way that leaves open the possibility of surprise and of encountering the unexpected.

FIELDS OF STUDY AND DEVELOPING RESEARCH QUESTIONS

All research starts with a problem or an issue to be explored and investigated. While ethnographic research draws on an understanding of developing ideas and theory through the systematic collection and analysis of data, it is still possible and indeed desirable to develop the problem a little before beginning the research proper. This can be done through engagement with existing data on or knowledge about the setting or comparable settings, exploring relevant or related literatures for concepts and phenomena that might be useful entrées into the setting, or starting from 'known facts' or 'assumed understandings' about a setting or phenomenon in order to generate 'how' and 'what' questions. Foreshadowing problems, issues or questions for exploration can provide the researcher with a practical way into a setting, from which ideas about how to explore and describe the setting might flow.

In ethnographic research it is usual to refer to the setting of investigation as the 'field' and the data collection undertaken as fieldwork. A field of study might refer to a physical location or institutional setting, but also to social or cultural space – a site in which and through which research is carried out – a particular organization such as a hospital, or school, or nightclub, or a public space such as the park, or train station or beach. And fieldwork here refers to the act of immersion in that setting, of 'doing' ethnography as an act of practice. Ethnographic research can be articulated in broader terms however, and it is possible to conduct excellent ethnographic research without immersion in a field of study – for example, by applying ethnographic principles to research activities that might include a series of conversations and encounters with social actors. Here the field might be the site from which the social actors come, and through them be the site of exploration – for example, a series of ethnographic conversations with midwives in order to understand midwifery practice, or listening to and conversing with teachers in the staffroom of a school in order to make sense of teachers' lives and selves in and out of school.

When a field of study is identified, pre-fieldwork practices or preliminary fieldwork can help to develop research questions and possible lines of inquiry. So, for example, undertaking some initial scoping research on the setting can often be possible and helpful. Collecting documents (see Rapley, 2018) in and of a setting can provide insights into the documentary realities of that setting, providing one way or indeed often multiple ways of 'seeing' and 'reading' a setting. Informal conversations and discussions, including exploring opportunities for access, might be possible, as might initial visits, some preliminary observation or the collection of visual images or sounds of the setting. Such activities actually mark the start of the research but can be usefully conceptualized as an initial or preliminary stage, enabling a more nuanced and focused research design to be developed, with the potential to scope out a range of lines of inquiry.

The field of study and research questions can also be developed out of our own interests and experiences, and completely legitimately so. A setting might well present itself in and through a personal experience. For example, there is a rich ethnographic tradition of teachers drawing on their experiences in undertaking school ethnographies (see Gordon et al., 2001, for an overview of ethnographic research in educational settings); equally, a number of sociologists have used their experiences of illness and health care settings to develop ethnographic analysis and insight on medical encounters and the body (see Beynon, 1987; Delamont, 1987; Horlick-Jones, 2011). The important thing here is that these personal experiences provide stimuli to engage ethnographically and reflexively with a field of study. They provide a way into and some important anchors for asking questions about the nature of experience and process. Indeed all ethnographic research builds on the resource of personal experience; by its very nature doing ethnography demands that the researcher is 'there' and, through personal engagement with the field, progressively focusing inquiry in order to develop rich descriptions and make sense of the field of study. So our personal interests and insights, to an extent at least, always guide our fieldwork practice, whether that be the stimuli for an initial interest in a topic or field of study, or through our personal reflections and experiences that enable fieldwork to become fine-tuned and detailed. The role of the ethnographic researcher in shaping and asking the questions, and in providing critical reflection is key. This does not assume a personalized, narcissistic or inward-facing research agenda. While the personal is intrinsic to the ethnographic project, it is important to acknowledge and question our own subjectivities and positionalities, drawing on but not being limited by our personal interests and questions.

METHODS OF DATA GENERATION

There are a range of methods for generating data in ethnographic research. Hence, ethnographic research design includes making choices about data types and ways of generating those data. To 'generate' is a term used here with purpose and on purpose. The term 'data collection' implies that there are data to be collected; data which are already 'out there', ripe and ready to be harvested. Data collection can sound like rather a passive process, with a neutral researcher moving through a field as a data collector. This does a disservice to the processes and practices of ethnography, to the role of the ethnographer researcher and indeed to the complexities of social life.

Data which might tell us something about the social world, and enable us to develop understandings about the life worlds of social actors demand a more active engagement on the part of the researcher. Data are not 'there', already in existence, simply to be collected up, organized and stored. Rather, ethnographic data are generated through various kinds of interaction with a social setting and/or social actors, crafted through our research practices. Indeed ethnographic data are all, in some way or another, co-productions between researchers, people in the field and the field itself. Data are made not caught.

The starting point for data generation for much ethnographic research is participant observation. This is where the researcher becomes a participant in the setting to a greater or lesser extent, in order to observe and record what is happening. Data in these circumstances, usually taking the form of fieldnotes, are made in situ during observation where possible, and expanded and developed after fieldwork. These data then are jottings and detailed notes, serving as a re-presentation of what has happened in the field. Participant observation is often held up as the gold standard for ethnographic data collection (see Atkinson and Coffey, 2002) and most clearly embodies key ethnographic research principles and the ethnographic spirit – being there, experiencing, watching, listening and feeling in order to understand and make sense. In ethnography there are different degrees to which participation in a setting is possible or desirable on the part of the researcher (see Gold, 1958, for a classical typology of researcher roles from participant through to observer; see also Chapter 5, this volume).

Participant observation can generate rich, layered data, but it can also demand a lengthy time commitment – sometimes stretching over several weeks, months, years or even decades (see Fowler and Hardesty, 1994; Okely and Callaway, 1992). This may influence the research design decisions that might or can be made. Time is an important factor to bear in mind. So too is the extent to which access to undertake participant observation can be successfully negotiated, as well as the ease or difficulty with which it might be possible to conduct observational fieldwork. In some settings, for example, being a participant observer in the setting may be dangerous, risky or impossible. It is worth noting here, however, that there is a long tradition of ethnographic participant observational fieldwork in settings that might have been initially considered difficult to access or dangerous or risky (see Nilan, 2002; Tewksbury, 2009).

Alongside, in addition to, or instead of participant observation, there are a range of other methods that usefully form part of the ethnographer's data generation tool kit. **Ethnographic interview**ing – conversations with a purpose (Burgess, 1984; see Brinkmann and Kvale, 2018) – is a widely used method, both taking advantage of and being situated within the narrative turn within the social sciences (Czarniawska, 2004).

Ethnographic interviewing builds on the anthropological approach to fieldwork – asking questions of social actors in the context of their everyday experiences, as part of participant observation. Interviewing, though, can also be utilized as an alternative to participant observation. Research can be ethnographic and be conducted through a series of extended interviews as conversations, and planned as such, recorded manually or digitally. Film also has a long history within ethnographic research, from the documentary style anthropological films of the early to mid-twentieth century through to a wider ranging visual revolution of the last few decades where still, moving and digital media have served to enhance and extend the repertoire of the ethnographic researcher for generating data for analysis. Ethnographic research design can include planning to generate researcher-produced still and moving images, supporting participants to create their own images, as well as gathering images of settings already created by participants or others (such visual data can include photographs and film, but also maps, pictures, digital media and other art forms). These approaches provide opportunities for differently generating data about social worlds. It is worthy of note here that digital technologies have also made it easier to capture the sounds of settings. Soundscapes can add a further sensory exploration of social life; noise and sound are very pertinent ways in which we experience and undertake our daily lives (Hall et al., 2008). The digital age has also brought with it new opportunities for data generation in ethnographic research. The digital landscape that encompasses websites, email communication, mobile phone technologies, geographical and mapping applications and social media means that there are a variety of ways in which social settings and social life are now digitally experienced, and through which researchers can engage with/in research settings. Ethnographic data can be gathered through participation in and engagement with these mediated technologies. This includes, for example, participant observation of virtual worlds, mobile and virtual interviews and the analysis of digital artefacts and documents of social life (Hine, 2000; Kozinets, 2009).

Gathering and generating digital data is an important way in which we can explore the documentary realities of the social settings we seek to understand. Documents, whether they be digital or otherwise, are also an important part of the ethnographic data repertoire and should be seriously considered in ethnographic research design. Early ethnographic research drawing on the anthropological tradition, was often undertaken in non-literate societies; while such societies did not rely on written texts, their daily lives were still documented through paintings, art work and material artefacts; in contemporary societies documents of various kinds can and do serve important functions, and can be used as part of the ways in which we seek to gain understandings about how a setting or organization operates and is organized, and how lives are lived (Plummer, 2001). As May notes, 'documents read as the sedimentation of social practices' and also 'constitute particular readings of social events' (2001, p. 176). Ethnographic researchers do not always recognize the potential of studying and generating documents and texts as data. In ethnographic research design it can be useful to consider the potential and possibilities of documents as data, not just to provide background to a setting but also as ways of understanding social practice.

In relation to research design, the process of data generation can be approached in two ways in ethnography. These approaches are not mutually exclusive. An ethnographic project can be designed with methods for data generation explicitly foregrounded and planned. For example, a research project can be planned from the outset to undertake ethnographic interviews with a number of **key informant**s, or with the explicit intention of generating a series of co-produced photographs, or with a clear plan to engage explicitly in participant observation appropriately signalled during access discussions with a research site. Equally, an ethnographic project can be initiated rather more broadly, with perhaps no more than a general plan to visit the setting and undertake some level of participant observation, open to the possibilities of utilizing complementary methods should the opportunity or perceived need arise. So, for example, through participating in the daily life of a setting it may become apparent that the sounds of a setting appear to offer particularly evocative ways of understanding and making sense of that setting, and hence soundscapes might become part of the data collection repertoire for the project. Or perhaps there occurs, through sustained engagement in the field, the opportunity to gather or generate photographic records of a setting; or it begins to seem relevant or important to complement observations and informal conversations with more formally planned and scheduled ethnographic interviews. Ethnographic data collection is always, at least in part, an iterative process, and justifiably so. It is helpful to think of ethnographic research design as a cyclical rather than a linear process, where data collection strategies are interwoven with the analytical attention we give our data and the ideas we generate during fieldwork (see Flick, 2018a).

ANALYSIS AND REFLECTION

In ideal circumstances the analytical strategy or strategies should be considered as part of the research design process. Data analysis should not be seen as a distinct stage of ethnographic research, separate from the processes of data collection or theorization. Rather, analysis is integral to the ethnographic research endeavour – a reflexive activity that helps to inform data collection and drives further fieldwork. Analysis is certainly not one of the last aspects of the ethnographic research process, undertaken after data collection has ended. Rather analysis is part of research design, and might actually be undertaken before as well as during and after data collection. Ahead of fieldwork and data collection, there might be initial analyses of existing materials, documents and so on, which will enable ideas and foreshadowed problems to be developed. During fieldwork, periods for reading data and having ideas about those data should be built in. Analysis as-you-go helps to shape ongoing fieldwork, enables the researcher to progressively focus the ethnographic gaze and encourages a reflexive approach to the ethnography as a holistic research process. Hence, there should be a fluid and dynamic relationship between data collection and data analysis in ethnography.

In simple terms analysis is concerned with having ideas about the research setting (see Gibbs, 2018). In relation specifically to research design, there are choices to be made concerning the strategies that are chosen in order to undertake data analysis; techniques that permit and enable close readings of data systematically and creatively. It is possible to identify strategies for data analysis at the start of a project and indeed it is wise to at least have in mind how data will be managed during the ethnographic project. Questions about analysis that might be asked as part of the research design include: how will data be recorded and organized? How will data generated as part of the project be stored? How will data be categorized and retrieved during the project? What form or forms will data take and what options are there for analysis? What analytical strategies might work best for interview data? Field notes? Visual data? How can computer software support data analysis – and what are the opportunities and constraints of using technologies to support analysis? A preference for a particular analytical strategy might drive the ways in which data are generated and stored. For example, if there is a preference for undertaking **narrative analysis**, for understanding a social setting or organization through attending to narrative structures and devices, then fieldwork will similarly need to pay attention to the collection of narratives, through perhaps verbatim recording of 'naturally occurring' interaction, or through ethnographic interviews, or through the collection of documents generated in and of the setting. Equally, analytical strategies might emerge over the course of fieldwork, as a response to data generated in the field. For example, it may be that there are opportunities that arise during fieldwork to generate or otherwise collect photographic data that will prompt an analytical strategy that supports the analysis of visual materials; or fieldwork might reveal particular or specialized vocabularies, not anticipated at the start of the research, which suggests that a close attention to language might be helpful, perhaps including some kind of semantic analysis.

There are no right or wrong ways to analyze data from ethnographic research projects. There is variety both in relation to what is meant or understood by analysis, and also in relation to the techniques that are available to manage, store and work with ethnographic data. What is important is that early attention is paid to the possibilities of data analysis, and to attendant imperatives that analytical choices might have for fieldwork, modes of data and for the organization of data. Analysis can refer primarily to data management and data handling – incorporating tasks such as organizing, sorting, indexing, coding, retrieving and classifying data. At this level, data analysis is reliant on systematic and procedural techniques, best put in place at the outset of the project. All analysis in ethnographic research involves some kind of close and detailed reading of data, and so it is vital that early attention is given to data organization and retrieval. There should be plans put in place early on to record and store data systemically, in ways that are efficient and effective for retrieval and close working. Practically speaking, this means building into the research process times to write up or transcribe data, to upload or otherwise store data, and to add indexation or organizational tools. Moreover, this data handling work is also an important way of having regular and ongoing interaction with data and periods of reflection, which are vital to shaping ongoing and future fieldwork. Ethnographic analysis can also refer to the creative and imaginative work of the ethnographer to interpret, interrogate and speculate, to interact with but also to go beyond the data. For ethnographic research design this means being open to the creation of spaces for working with and on the data during the fieldwork process, ensuring there are times for ideas emergent from data to be developed, tested, elaborated and reworked during the research. Analysis in this sense then involves an ongoing dialogue with and between data and ideas.

KEY POINTS

- Ethnography is particularly suitable for addressing research topics and questions concerned with process and practice.
- The process of undertaking research in ethnography is usually referred to as fieldwork. Fieldwork can include a variety of methods for generating data.
- Participant observation is a main method for conducting ethnographic research.
- The ethnographic research process is non-linear; research design should recognize that data collection and data analysis are not discrete activities.
- Strategies for data collection and data analysis can be planned in advance as part of research design in ethnography. They can also emerge during the research process.
- Data organization and management should be considered as part of research design in ethnographic research.

◼ FURTHER READING

Fetterman, D.M. (2009) *Ethnography: Step by Step*, 3rd ed. Thousand Oaks, CA: Sage.

LeCompte, M.D. and Schensul, J.J. (2010) *Designing and Conducting Ethnographic Research*, 2nd ed. Lanham, MD: AltaMira Press.

Murchison, J. (2010) *Ethnography Essentials: Designing, Conducting and Presenting Your Research*. San Francisco, CA: Jossey Bass.

CHAPTER THREE

SITES, CASES AND PARTICIPANTS

CONTENTS

OBJECTIVES

After reading this chapter, you will:

- have an appreciation of how personal circumstances, characteristics and our sense of self impact upon ethnographic fieldwork choices;
- be able to identify a range of factors that are taken into consideration when choosing a site for ethnographic study;
- understand how ethnographers can sample within a field site and select participants; and
- be able to describe key factors in successfully securing access to the field.

STARTING FROM WHERE YOU ARE

Choosing a site or setting for ethnographic study can depend on wide range of factors, and time should be taken to consider the various options that might be available to you. There are some considerations that will be pragmatic rather than necessarily intellectual. For example, engagement in ethnographic research can be time consuming, so in some circumstances it might be preferable to select a research setting in near proximity to your work or home; where research can more readily fit in around study, employment or domestic commitments. Ethnographic research does not need or require physical distance in order to be intellectually interesting. There will be many settings 'close to home' that offer promising sites for ethnographic exploration. Equally, an opportunity to engage in ethnographic study might be presented simply by being in the right place at the right time, perhaps due to an existing relationship with an organization or group of people, or through a personal introduction from a friend or acquaintance. There may also be some potential research settings where it might be difficult to undertake participant observation because of your own personal characteristics, or views. While the role of an ethnographer is to understand settings and social worlds from the perspective of those who are within those settings (and where the capacity to set aside one's own views is important), there might be some cultural settings where the views held or actions undertaken are so at odds with your own that it would be too difficult or distressing for you to undertake the research. As we have noted, ethnographic research does involve a personal commitment and researcher presence in the field. Thus, protecting our own emotional or physical wellbeing must be a consideration in our fieldwork choices. Furthermore, while we can control some aspects of our personal self during and as part of fieldwork – for example, how we speak, dress and act – it is not always possible to control other aspects of our identity – for example, our race or age. Such personal characteristics might make research difficult or impossible in some circumstances – for example, where those aspects of identity are particularly salient to that setting. So, in choosing where and with whom to undertake ethnographic research it is important that we start from 'where we are' and 'who we are', recognizing that the most important tool in ethnographic research is the researcher. This does not mean ruling out 'difficult' settings right from the outset, but it does demand the development of a self-conscious approach to fieldwork choices. There needs to be awareness of the ways in which our personal self does and will interact with the field. Reflexivity is a key aspect of ethnographic research, attending to the effect of the researcher on the research process and in the context of knowledge production. This means careful and ongoing consideration of the position of the researcher in relation to the research setting, and through all stages of the research journey – including before the commencement of fieldwork, as well as during fieldwork. This self-awareness should not limit the opportunities of and for fieldwork or for the selection of sites for research, but must form a backdrop to what is possible.

SELECTING A FIELD SITE

There are a number of considerations that are brought to bear in choosing where and with whom to undertake ethnographic research (see Flick, 2018a). It is very rare indeed that a setting simply presents itself for analysis, and for the researcher there will always be options and choices. The range of factors that it might be useful to take into account in selecting a field site include:

1   *The topic or research question under focus:* Field sites are selected on the basis that they seem as though they will or may provide opportunities to explore the topic or question of focus in a clear and defined way, or indeed in an interesting or creative way. Field sites will ideally offer exemplars and opportunities for exploration, perhaps in a range of ways. While it might be difficult to fully appreciate the possibilities of fieldwork ahead of it actually starting, settings that appear to speak to your research interest, offering a number of cases or participants, in which and through which the topic of interest can be studied, are worthy of consideration.

2   *Access considerations:* Almost all field sites require some form of access negotiation, agreement or permission. We need to be able to 'get into' the setting in order to undertake fieldwork. Sometimes formal permission or indeed permissions will be required, perhaps from a range of actors from within a setting. Finding out who to ask, and anticipating how requests to undertake research might be received can be an important part of gaining understandings of settings. In some cases informal support and sponsorship will be required, or will be a great help in securing access. Some settings will require both formal and informal access agreements, and indeed ongoing access negotiations. Even settings or sites that might be perceived as 'public' are not exempt from questions of access. Indeed starting fieldwork, overtly or covertly, in public arenas raises particular ethical contexts that require thoughtful consideration. Thinking through how easy or difficult it might be to gain access to a setting definitely needs to be taken into account when making fieldwork choices, though such considerations should not unduly limit our ambition to study settings that on the face of it might be difficult or challenging to access. Understanding how to get into a setting or field site and who can help is actually an important part of the research process, and in itself can be revealing of the setting.

3   *The opportunity for comparability and/or unique exploration:* All social research builds on what has gone before, in some way or another. In selecting a research setting for ethnographic study it is appropriate to be mindful of the contribution that will be made to an existing body of research and knowledge. For example, a setting might be selected for inquiry precisely because it is different to sites that have been explored in previous research, perhaps enabling common research questions to be applied to and explored in new environments. Equally, a setting might well be selected because it actually is, or appears to be, the same as or very similar to settings studied in previous research. Here the new contribution to knowledge might be, for example, exploring a different focus, comparison over time, new foreshadowed research questions, or a different sample of informants. It is this variation that presents an opportunity for original but comparable exploration. In choosing a setting, it is important to appreciate the ways in which individual research projects speak to the wider body of research, and to be mindful how new research will add to our understandings. The choice of research setting will not determine the contribution your ethnographic project might make to existing work, but will provide an important frame of reference.

4   *Fitting in and getting on:* Ethnographic research depends upon the researcher being able to engage with the site of exploration, and to have ongoing opportunities to interact with participants (which might include observation, listening

and asking questions). There are a number of positions that ethnographers can adopt in the field (see Chapter 5, this volume), requiring or facilitating different levels of participation and interaction. Thinking about your possible role, or roles in the field – how you will be perceived, how easy or difficult it might be to be undertake fieldwork and the ways in which your presence may impact upon the setting – are important considerations in choosing a field site. Settings should ideally be selected where it is possible (or likely at least) for the ethnographer to adopt a role or roles that permit participant observation and/or conversation, while keeping disruption to the setting to a minimum. However, not selecting a setting just because it is not immediately obvious how fieldwork can be conducted is also unhelpful. What is important here is that early attention is paid in relation to how fieldwork will be conducted – the possibilities as well as the challenges, and how these might be managed. Of course, over the course of fieldwork it may be possible, desirable or necessary to adopt a variety of roles in order to manage relations in the field.

5   *Initial exploration and pre-fieldwork:* It is sometimes possible to carry out initial early research in or around a possible research setting. This can be used to develop foreshadowed problems, test out the practical possibilities of undertaking fieldwork and develop suitable strategies for accessing the field proper. It might also be the case that there are a number of possible settings to choose from. In which case, some preliminary fieldwork can be used to assess the options. Pre-fieldwork might include visiting the setting once or on more than one occasion, having conversations ('interviews') with social actors in the field who are readily accessible (or are not in or of the setting but have knowledge of and experience in the setting, or of similar settings) and collecting readily available data on and from the setting – for example, public documents, photographs and so forth. Such pre-fieldwork can inform the choice of setting and assist with planning data collection strategies, as well as helping to further develop the research problem or foreshadowed questions.

6   *Happenstance and a degree of luck:* The above considerations are all helpful in providing some pointers towards systematically selecting a setting in which to undertake an ethnographic study. It should be noted, however, that in some instances a setting might present itself for study even prior to the formulation of research questions or the identification of a foreshadowed problem. Sometimes opportunities present themselves (or are foisted upon us) with respect to the site of study. Sometimes we just happen to be 'here' or 'there', and that seems as good a place as any to begin an ethnographic journey. This may be a setting which we are familiar with, and are 'at home' in, in our everyday lives. For example,

teacher practitioners undertaking research in their own school settings, or other professional groups studying the everyday work settings in which they operate, or ethnographic 'patients' finding themselves in a position where they can generate rich ethnographic data through their own experiences of illness (Horlick-Jones, 2011; Kolker, 1996; Paget, 1993). Similarly, there might be a chance encounter (a meeting, an unexpected visit, an experience in our personal lives) or a throwaway remark ('you should come and research us here', 'let me know if you need an introduction'), which sparks an interest or provides a platform for thinking about doing research in a specific setting. In such circumstances the setting might be 'selected' ahead of a particular set of research questions or ideas for areas of study. The setting might just seem interesting or unusual or accessible or welcoming or convenient, and it is through early exposure to the setting that issues to be explored will be identified. This is not so very different from what happens in any case, for all the careful planning and initial development of topics and questions to be explored. It is usually through our initial and early fieldwork experiences in the setting or by talking to people within that setting that we start to progressively focus our ideas for ethnographic exploration.

SELECTING CASES AND CHOOSING INFORMANTS

It is perhaps a little misplaced to focus too much on the general setting or settings chosen for study, as it is in fact what or who is studied within those settings that is of most significance to the ethnographer. While we might define our study in terms of the setting or 'field', it is important to remember that settings or 'fields' are of themselves socially and culturally constituted; settings are not static or fixed phenomena but rather are dynamic and negotiated spaces for activity and interaction. Thus a setting or field can be defined and studied in a variety of ways, in relation to the cases that are chosen for focus and the social actors that are observed or spoken to. And, in turn, it may be that in order to explore a case or the experience of a social actor in detail, we might need to transcend the boundaries of settings – working across and between settings or fields of study. In simple terms, it is not possible to study everything in a setting in order to arrive at a definitive and full description. In order to study a setting and to come to an ethnographically informed understanding of that setting, we draw on a range of illustrative examples for description and analysis; we select cases and informants to provide ways into a setting, and to help us develop insight into and understanding of the field. A setting provides an ethnographic context in which and through which we can explore (always) selected lives, actions and events. In selecting cases and informants we might be mindful of explorations of both similarity and contrast. That is, we might choose cases and informants which appear to be the same or similar. Equally, we might purposefully base our selection on points of difference.

The selection of cases and informants makes explicit the ways in which ethnography provides opportunities to progressively focus through careful and systematic selection of people, events, activities and actions to be explored. Such selection stops a taken-for-granted notion of a research setting as naturally occurring, or of data simply 'there' to be collected; instead there is an imperative on the part of the ethnographer to play an active role in identifying and defining cases and informants in an attempt to draw together and generate data that will enable sense to be made of the setting.

Theoretical sampling provides one way of approaching the exercise of selecting cases for exploration (Glaser and Strauss, 1967; see also Flick, 2018d). Theoretical sampling encourages cases to be identified in order to generate as many categories as possible, thus giving maximum scope to develop and test emergent theoretical assumptions. Cases for exploration might be selected in order to explore similarities and differences, whereby cases are identified that provide aspects of comparison and contrast within a setting. Equally, it might be possible to identify a range of cases for investigation based on a developing understanding of a setting – considering, for example, the different contexts, arenas for activity, places and sites for interaction that operate within a setting. So, for example, if the ethnographic focus is on describing and developing understanding of the everyday social worlds of a hospital setting, then selected cases for study might be different wards or specialties which provide context, or different regions and spaces where hospital work gets done, or different arenas of hospital activity. This might be undertaken within a single given hospital, or across a range of different hospital settings. The point here is that sampling cases provides a way of managing fieldwork and of focusing our activity and interest. At the same time the selection of cases is fieldwork, as the act itself relies on emergent understandings of the field setting.

Selecting cases implies 'sampling' within a setting in order to provide units for detailed data collection and analysis; 'samples' provide proxies for a setting rather than representing the setting in any kind of complete way. Cases enable manageable opportunities for exploring the setting, usually from a range of perspectives and viewpoints. There is, and can be, no intention that cases are representative of the setting as a whole. Indeed the only way to 'represent' a setting completely would be to study the whole setting in all its facets, and that is simply not possible – given that all settings are socially and culturally constituted, will be experienced differently by the same people, and in similar ways by different people, and are constantly evolving, shifting and being reconstituted.

As ethnographers we also sample within cases, in order to further focus our research endeavours. Such sampling decisions form important parts of the research process; making decisions about how to approach a setting or a case within a setting relies upon a developing knowledge and understanding. We must decide who to talk to, when to talk to them and what questions to ask of them. We must choose what to observe and/or participate in, when to observe, when to join in and when not to. We also make sampling decisions in relation to what information to record, as well as when to record and how to record our observations and conversations. The ways in which we sample, as we refine and progressively focus our research, will be subject to change over the course of any project, as knowledge of the setting evolves and research questions are framed. It is worthy of note that there is a necessary balance to be struck between careful planning, enabling systematic and progressive focusing, and those unforeseen or opportune moments in ethnographic fieldwork that take us by surprise and lead us in directions we simply had not thought of. Both are vital to ethnographic research, we can plan for the former, but we must also anticipate the latter.

Choosing cases and sampling within cases is something that will happen over the course of an ethnographic project; this work cannot all be planned upfront and ahead of the research starting. However, there are some useful things that can be borne in mind, in scoping out how to approach the selection of cases within a setting.

- *Who to include:* Social actors – people – provide one axis for sampling within a setting. There are three main ways of undertaking the selection of potential participants or informants within a case:

    1   Through a designed sampling frame based on demographic or other known characteristics about social actors in a setting that are or can be readily accessible. These might be generic categories such as gender, age or ethnicity, or they can be case specific – for example, the occupation or grade within a particular work setting. While using such criteria might be a useful starting point, such strategic sampling is only really useful if these categories are overtly apparent or emergent as important to making sense of the setting that is the subject of ethnographic inquiry.

    2   Through identifying categories defined by social actors themselves within the case. Lofland (1976) usefully referred to these as 'member-identified categories'; taxonomies of terms used by social actors to describe or label types of people within the setting. Such sampling might only become possible

during the course of fieldwork, as the ethnographer starts to get to know the setting and 'hear' the situated vocabularies of social actors within the setting.

3   Through constructing ethnographer-led categories or 'types' of people through initial data collection and analysis, which in turn provides a framework from which to strategically sample informants. This approach can be developed through preliminary or ongoing observations and conversations, and in relation to initial analysis and developing understandings of the setting. For example, over the course of a project social actors might be identified in relation to the levels of knowledge and experience that they demonstrate or otherwise bring to a setting. We might be able to begin to categorize members as newcomers, 'old hands', experienced, rebels, conformers, those that are vocal, those that are quiet, and so forth. In such circumstances it is important that we remain mindful of testing our common-sense understandings, of ensuring we don't take for granted those categories we are generating and of being open to revising and rethinking how we are identifying potential participants as our research progresses.

*   *When to study:* Temporality provides a potentially useful framework from which to sample within a case. It sounds an obvious thing to say that social and cultural life is experienced through and in time. However, the ways in which time structures experiences, events and actions is often overlooked (Adam, 1990). All settings, as fields of study, have temporal structures which can provide a conceptual lens through which we might gain detailed understanding. To take a straightforward example of, perhaps, a primary or elementary school setting, experiencing that primary school at different times of day will generate different understandings of what goes on in that ordinary school setting. What is typically thought of as the 'school day' itself (when children are present) is relatively short compared to the time the school building is actually open and 'peopled'– by teachers, caretakers, school cooks and administrative staff at work, or by community groups using the school buildings and facilities 'after hours'. If you were to visit the school in the morning, before the school bell rings and the school day begins for the children, there might be a playground full of parents dropping off children, with teachers leading lines of children into school. At other times the playground will be empty or being used for structured activity. The playing out of school relations take on particular forms and functions over the course of the day. Inside the school building Monday mornings might 'look' and 'feel' differently to Friday afternoons. We can scale up this temporal lens to think about the rhythms of a whole school year. For example, visitors to a primary school setting in the UK in the lead up to the Christmas holidays would come away with

a very particular impression of an 'ordinary' school schedule (involving nativity plays, making snowmen out of cotton wool, and lots of glitter art), and certainly a very different one from what might take place on a wet afternoon in March, or the last week of the summer term before the summer holidays. The point here is not that the ethnographer needs to study a setting at all times of day or on all days of the year in order to fully understand or appreciate its social and cultural milieu. Rather, it is to note that an awareness of the temporal organization of a setting, and of the ways in which an organization imposes or lives by rhythm, provides the opportunity to develop temporal sampling frames from which cases might be selected for detailed exploration and attention. Some of this work – of selecting cases by or through time might be possible ahead of starting ethnographic fieldwork. For example, as part of pre-fieldwork it might be useful to think through how time and temporality impacts upon a setting, and how our observations and conversations might work to explore and capture the different rhythms of everyday life. More likely, it is during fieldwork that we might come to understand something of the temporal organization of a setting, which may in turn lead us to purposively select cases (times) for exploration. There will be particular times which present as particularly significant or interesting – for example, times of and for transition, quiet times, busy times, times when lots seems to happen, and times when 'nothing happens'. Of course 'nothing never happens', and it is important that in the selection of cases we include the seemingly routine or 'ordinary' times rather than just times which appear particularly eventful or extraordinary.

- *Where to research:* Settings are rarely, if ever, homogeneous and constant spaces. Rather most if not all settings will have a number of spatially defined areas and regions, perhaps associated with different activities and/or people. Social actors may behave differently in different spaces within a setting, and these different spaces will also provide a range of contexts within which everyday activity takes place. Goffman's (1959) distinction of 'backstage' and 'frontstage' is a helpful analogy here. Such a distinction provides a mechanism through which we can articulate the ways in which social life is something akin to performance, with 'back regions' as well as 'front of house' practices and performances. Of course, the point here is not that there are some aspects of social life that are 'fabricated' (i.e. self-consciously performed in ways that render them artificial), and some aspects which are more authentic or real. Rather, it is to recognize the spatial and indeed other contexts in which events, behaviours and actions are taking place. For example, hospital surgical staff may behave differently in the operating theatre with an unconscious patient, to how they may act during a busy ward round.

Equally, a secondary school staffroom will provide a different perspective on the everyday work and social relations of teachers to that of the classroom setting; or the spectacle of a graduation ceremony will provide a very different view on the work of a university, from observing a committee in progress or attending a first year undergraduate class. Social actors also behave differently in different company within the social spaces they occupy. Our social roles are socially constructed differently in relation to other roles and relationships. A school classroom will have a different dynamic from 'usual' if the head teacher or an external inspector is present, so too will the school staffroom. Colleagues in an office setting may go about their work differently depending on whether the CEO is in the building. Again, it is important to emphasize that an awareness of the spaces and spatial contexts of settings should not imply an unrealistic expectation that all areas can or should be studied or sampled as part of an ethnographic project. That is simply not possible even if it were desirable. Identifying and coming to recognize the ways in which social life is spatially experienced, and social settings spatially contextualized, can be an outcome of ethnographic research. An understanding of the spatial and place-making contexts in which people act can also be built into the selection of cases to be explored.

GETTING IN – ACCESSING THE FIELD

However cases and participants are selected, ethnographic research is dependent upon gaining access to settings and to people. As Bailey (1996) states, gaining entry can be a complicated business. While it is important that the researcher thinks carefully and reflexively about the selection of settings, participants and cases, in practice what is possible is very much dependent on whether our selections are open for and to study, and on successfully negotiating access. Initial access to a setting and/or to participants is crucial and can determine the course of the whole project. However, it needs to be acknowledged that access is often (and most usually) an ongoing process throughout ethnographic research. Research access, as in permission to carry out the research and secure the cooperation of participants, is often conceptualized as a 'problem' or challenge to be managed and overcome. It is perhaps more productive to think of access as an integral part of the research process itself, often subject to ongoing negotiation and renegotiation (Burgess, 1991). How and in what ways we gain access to a setting or to our informants can actually tell us quite a lot about that setting, how it is organized and the roles of social actors within the setting.

Negotiating research access is rarely as simple as just asking permission. But in many settings there will be formal or less formal structures to be navigated, and various 'official' permissions to be asked for and granted (or not). Working out who to ask or who needs to be asked (and in what ways) is part and parcel of the research process, and comes with a developing level of understanding about the setting. It may be that there are 'official' organizational structures in place, that require acknowledgement in some way, perhaps with a formal approach for institutional 'permission' to conduct fieldwork within an organization. This is, of course, important (and can be crucial), but is rarely enough to secure access. Formal permissions are different from the 'on the ground' consent that may be required from social actors in order for an ethnographer to participate in a social setting, and to generate and record data from that setting. In some settings – for example, public or semi-public settings – it may even not be immediately obvious that there are permissions to be asked, and if so who to ask. And yet gaining meaningful access to activities, events and people will still require careful negotiation or action. Gaining access through 'hanging out', 'joining in' or through establishing relationships still involves permission of sorts, it is still necessary to be able to articulate and account for your presence in the field, and to ensure that your research practice is ethical and mindful of wellbeing and issues of informed consent.

In many settings successfully negotiating access to undertake ethnographic research will rely upon or benefit from key individuals or groups. It may be possible to identify effective **gatekeeper**s to a setting. Gatekeepers are social actors that are able to provide a way into a setting; they might informally or formally police access to a particular organization or social group and be able to facilitate introductions to others in the field. They might vouch for you, watch out for you, provide you with 'inside' information, or act as a sponsor or key informant. It may be possible to identify gatekeepers ahead of starting fieldwork, drawing on your existing or introductory knowledge of the setting. It is more usual, perhaps, for gatekeepers or sponsors to emerge during initial fieldwork, or indeed over the course of ethnographic research. Over a prolonged project, the numbers of key informants who work with you or are supportive of you might grow; new sponsors might emerge, enabling access to new aspects and perspectives of the field. Sponsorship can be hugely beneficial to the progress of an ethnographic project, and can be a key factor in choosing sites, cases and informants. However, it is important to remain reflexive of the ways in which sponsorship can shape your research and the ways in which you are perceived in the field. Being seen to be particularly closely associated to some people in the field, rather than to others, might close off access to others with contrastive views or alternative positions. There are risks too in becoming especially persuaded by particular views of everyday practice in the field, to the possible exclusion of other perspectives and voices.

Gatekeepers or sponsors will have their own sets of social relations in the field, which will help to shape the ethnographers' interactions both with them and with others. There may be vested interests at stake, or perhaps clear or more nuanced power relations. Such reflections do not imply that we should be suspicious of individuals or groups in the field who are supportive of our research and are helpful in opening doors for us. Rather, relationships with sponsors or key informants should be managed with sensitivity and reflection, mindful of what these relationships might tell us about the social and cultural settings we are seeking to understand, mindful too of the possibilities and limits that such sponsorship might provide.

Getting into a setting also requires the ethnographer to be able to articulate their research to people in the setting; to describe what they are interested in and what they will be doing in ways that are meaningful to social actors in the setting. In some instances the researcher might encounter reluctance, refusal or resistance from potential research participants. In such cases access might be a long-term project requiring careful management. Bengry-Howell and Griffin (2012) describe the ways in which ethnographers can be charged with implicit persuasion on occasion, in order to gain access. In all cases we must provide a script of our research – or indeed scripts, as we may need to describe our research differently in order to explain ourselves to different audiences within the field. This involves thinking carefully about how to describe our research plans; this can be particularly challenging in ethnographic work where there might be a legitimate lack of clarity in relation to the focus for the research, or on how the data generation and analysis will develop. There will be occasions when information will need to be differently presented, and where perhaps limited information is initially shared – for example, where there might be sensitivities or uncertainties that would be best articulated once good fieldwork relationships have been established. Sometimes ethnographic research begins covertly, either where we retrospectively recognize we have been participating in a setting that becomes ethnographically interesting to us, or where purposive research is started and the researcher role is only revealed once field relations are established. As Hammersley and Atkinson (2007) note, **covert research** brings with it a whole host of ethical considerations and anxieties, as well as a range of practical difficulties. Deception should be avoided wherever possible. More usually, there is often less of a demarcation between early pre-fieldwork and the beginning of research proper than we might think. And our scripts, of what we are researching and why, might develop and change, as we establish ourselves in the field and develop a clearer understanding of what we are interested in and how best to explain it to participants in ways that are appropriate.

One of the key characteristics of successful ethnography is the capacity of the researcher to build trust and rapport with social actors in the research setting. This is not always easy to do, and needs to be considered as a key and ongoing part of the research process. Establishing rapport and trust is something to be worked on and at, over the course of our ethnographic encounters. Developing such relations is not necessarily something that researchers are 'just' naturally good at. Rapport needs to be worked on, and in ways that are sensitive to different social actors in the field. This involves sensitively reading the social landscape and actively seeking ways to 'get on' with people, including those you might not necessarily feel a natural affinity with. There are also risks associated with over-rapport, where becoming very or overly close to study participants may bring its own difficulties; for example, if you are perceived as taking on some viewpoints and not others, and of sharing fieldwork moments with some participants to the exclusion of others (Coffey, 1999).

There are no rules to developing good rapport in the field, but there are a number of things to consider. For example, it is best not to make assumptions about what to expect, or what participants will think you already know. It is helpful to build rapport reciprocally where possible, in ways that are mutually meaningful. We should be honest about the extent to which we can participate in everyday practice, or for how long. And be clear when we will and will not be around. And where they are known, it is important to follow norms and conventions that are culturally relevant to the setting and appropriate to your status (for example, in relation to your age or gender). Being reflexive about the possibilities and challenges of building rapport is not just important as a 'way in' to do fieldwork, it is key to fieldwork itself, and to making sense of the social settings we seek to understand.

Access to a setting also requires consideration of the role or roles you are going to present and adopt in the field. There are often practical considerations to address in terms of managing your personal front during fieldwork (for example, in relation to your physical appearance, dress, language and so on). Your personal characteristics might also limit the roles you are able to play in the field. It is not possible, for example, to take on the role of child in a school when you are most clearly an adult. Equally, there are choices in relation to how far you feel able or are willing to participate in the setting, and also choices in relation to the kinds of impression management that you want or feel able to undertake. Within a setting you might adopt a number of roles, either with different people or over time; for example, confidante, friend, fellow worker, naïve incompetent, researcher, supporter and academic researcher. Ethnographic fieldwork cannot be accomplished without attention to the roles of the researcher, and such attention begins with how you initially present and develop your role during access and entry to a setting. In some circumstances a role may present itself or be pre-existing. In other circumstances much more thought may need to be given to ways of presenting and being in the field, both initially and as fieldwork progresses.

KEY POINTS

- Selecting a site for ethnographic study can include both intellectual and pragmatic considerations.
- There are a range of factors that can inform the choice of setting, including the research question, the ease with which access can be negotiated, the possibility for comparable study and the possibility for researcher engagement.
- The selection of cases and informants is a key part of ethnographic research. The aim is not to be representative, but to provide ways of systematically exploring the setting from a range of perspectives.
- Sampling in ethnographic work can take into account a range of factors including time, space and people. We can select cases in relation to the temporal rhythms of the setting, its physical regions, different activities that take place and the participants that operate within the field.
- Access is a term used to describe the process of seeking 'permissions' to undertake ethnographic study. This includes both formal requests that might be required, but also the informal ways in which the researcher seeks support, acceptance and cooperation from social actors in the field.
- Access in ethnographic work is a continual process rather than a one-off event, and includes the building of trust and the establishment of rapport.

FURTHER READING

Bengry-Howell, A. and Griffin, C. (2012) 'Negotiating access in ethnographic research with "hard to reach" young people: establishing common ground or a process of methodological grooming?', *International Journal of Social Research Methodology*, 15 (5): 403–16.
Brewer, J.D. (2009) *Ethnography*. Buckingham: Open University Press.
Small, M.L. (2009) 'On science and the logic of case selection in field-based research', *Ethnography*, 10 (1): 5–38.

CHAPTER FOUR

IN THE FIELD

OBSERVATION, CONVERSATION AND DOCUMENTATION

CONTENTS

OBJECTIVES

After reading this chapter, you will:

- understand the significance of initial fieldwork encounters and first days in the field;
- be able to describe main methods for data collection in ethnographic research;
- understand how to generate field notes from participant observation, recognising their qualities as textual productions;
- be able to describe the main features of ethnographic interviews and how they can be used in fieldwork; and
- have an appreciation of the role documents and multimodal data can play in ethnographic research.

MAKING DATA

Ethnographic research relies on the act of the researcher 'being there' as a key aspect of data collection. While much can be, and indeed often is gleaned by a careful analysis of documents in and of the field, the experience of fieldwork – as ethnographic practice – remains an important and core way in which we come to understand social settings and the lives of social actors. Principal data collection techniques used in ethnographic fieldwork practice are observation and conversation; that is drawing on our everyday practices of watching, asking and listening in order to perceive, understand and interpret the activities, events, actions, interactions and relationships of the setting under study. These methods of data gathering require an active engagement on the part of the researcher; indeed it is through sustained interaction with and observation of the setting and people within that setting that data are produced. Production implies a kind of purposeful practice; ethnographic data are made not 'caught'. That is, ethnographic data are co-productions by the researcher and the field of study. This does not, of course, mean that data are 'made up' in any crude or underhand sense. The good researcher applies a careful and systematic approach to working and interacting with the setting in order to document and describe. It does, though, imply that the role and work of the ethnographic researcher is key, in terms of what is observed, what is asked, what is heard and what is recorded.

INITIAL FIELDWORK AND FIRST DAYS IN THE FIELD

Ethnographic fieldwork begins from the very moment we enter a field setting, or indeed even before we enter a setting. In order to gain access to a setting it is usual to perhaps do some preliminary visits, or read up on the setting or have some 'informal' conversations with people who are in, or have knowledge of, the setting which will be the focus of the study. These pre-fieldwork events can be essential initial encounters – perhaps challenging early preconceptions we might have about a setting or providing early information about a setting when we are at our most perceptive or receptive as 'newcomers'. First days in the field (Geer, 1964) can be the most challenging and the most rewarding days of fieldwork for a whole variety of reasons. As someone potentially new to a setting, there will be an initial strangeness that the researcher can use to good effect. Where a social world, activity or group of people are unfamiliar to us in our everyday lives and encounters, we draw on all our everyday practices to 'make sense'; in the same way the ethnographic researcher who is new to a setting can bring a methodological naïvety to the research encounter, meaning they are in a position to absorb information without judgement, take 'everything in', observe what is happening without interpretation and ask those simple questions that might be unthinkable to someone who is perceived to be knowledgeable about or familiar with a setting. Of course we don't always research settings that are 'strange' to us; in which case early fieldwork needs to challenge what we think we know and provide a way to approach the setting with fresh eyes. The act of systematically observing and recording what is happening sounds straightforward enough, but can be especially difficult in settings where we think we already know 'what happens'. In this context it is useful to think about strategies to make the familiar strange. We have to work hard to see things afresh, and to tune in rather than tune out. In our everyday world we are very effective and efficient at focusing – screening out an awful lot of what goes on around us. As an ethnographer, first days in the field require us to draw on our senses in purposive and self-conscious ways in order to see familiar settings as a stranger might. The distinction between familiarity and strangeness has long been a feature of ethnographic work (see Geer, 1964; Becker, 1971; authors from the Second Chicago School of sociology who reflected a tradition of the trope of the stranger–observer, and of the difficulties of adopting such a persona in research 'at home' and/or in familiar places), though such a distinction is not as starkly drawn as we might think (Atkinson et al., 2003). Ethnographic research in all settings involves being reflexive about the experiences and knowledges that we bring to a setting, while not making taken-for-granted assumptions over what we think we know about a setting. A purpose of ethnographic fieldwork is to develop understanding of settings with which we are not familiar *and*, equally, to make sense of those social contexts with which we assume a level of cultural competence. A task of ethnographic practice is to not to rely on assumptions of what we think we know, with settings that are familiar *or* strange to us.

One challenge is how to record our initial observations and conversations – when faced with a blank page (literally or metaphorically) and an imperative to capture 'everything that is going on', not least in order to challenge any preconceived ideas or taken-for-granted assumptions that we might bring to the field. Of course, not everything can be recorded, so straightaway it is important to be self-conscious and aware of the focusing you will 'naturally' be doing, so as not to focus without thinking, and to develop strategies for refocusing, particularly in those early days of fieldwork when we won't know what is significant and what is not, for making sense of the specific social context. Another challenge is that, while wanting to record 'everything', we might feel that we struggle to see anything 'noteworthy' or worthy of recording, particularly in settings where we assume a level of cultural competence. A good mantra to be reminded of is that 'nothing never happens'. In making sense of social settings we are concerned with the very ordinariness of social and cultural life, not only with extraordinary events and happenings. Our task is to unravel and understand how the ordinary, mundane and business as usual is accomplished, through which the extraordinary or the unusual are contextualized. Approaching initial fieldwork – our first days in the field – with an open mind rather than an empty mind is key. An empty mind implies that data will appear out of nowhere and will find their way to our notebooks without any effort on the part of the researcher. An open mind recognizes and harnesses our existing assumptions and perceptions, but means we are attuned to being surprised, are excited by the everyday accomplishments of social and cultural life and develop practical and intellectual strategies to focus and refocus, to travel a line between and across the positions of familiarity and strangeness. It cannot be overstated that our early fieldwork experiences have an impact on our final analysis. The strategies and concepts we adopt and develop during our first days in the field will have an impact on future fieldwork and on the ways in which analysis and conceptualization progresses. In practical terms this means an early and ongoing alertness to our own preconceptions, an openness to being surprised, and clear strategies for recording and challenging initial observations.

PARTICIPANT OBSERVATION AND FIELD NOTES

Participant observation is an important part of the ethnographic repertoire. Participant observer is a role adopted by the ethnographer in order to gather data about a setting. There are a range of participant roles that can be adopted, along a continuum from complete participant through to non-participant observer (see Chapter 5 for more on roles and relationships in the field). In practice, most ethnographers partially participate in the setting, joining in to a greater or lesser extent, occupying a position of 'being there' and of interacting in and with a setting in order to observe and make sense of activities, events and relationships. Observation begins from the moment the researcher encounters the field, or indeed before fieldwork proper when initial meetings or visits might take place. Of course observation is not a neutral activity, nor can or should it be seen as objective in the sense of being detached from the participant observer. We bring to the field our personal characteristics and backgrounds, as well as our ideas, assumptions, experiences and theories. Good ethnographers are reflective of who they are and about what they bring to the field, how they might impact upon the field, and of the need for continuous and constructive challenge to ensure things are not missed or overlooked because of the experiences, characteristics and beliefs which they bring with them.

Observation begins by taking in as much as possible by watching and listening in a setting, recording what is happening in a detailed and systematic way. Structuring our observations in ways that prevent us overly focusing on one area or another, especially at the start of a project, is important. This is where sampling within a setting is useful, undertaking observation, for example, at different times, in different regions of the setting, or with different groups of people. Over time, as we become familiar with the setting, and as we start to have ideas about what is going on and how people are relating and interacting, observation can and should become progressively focused. This focus might shift and change over the course of prolonged fieldwork, as we come to identify various patterns of practice that will help us to gain understanding; that is, the range of actions, events, behaviours and interactions that demarcate and typify the setting. During fieldwork it is sometimes easy to get distracted by the spectacular or the unusual or the shocking. These aspects of a setting are more readily identifiable, can seem easier to document and record (because 'something is happening') and can be distracting, taking our attention away from practices that appear to be more mundane. The skill of a good ethnographer is to recognize and value, ethnographically speaking, what is usual and ordinary to a setting; and to be able to situate and contextualize occurrences that seem, to us, extraordinary in relation to what they might tell us about the 'business as usual' aspects of a setting.

The usual way of recording observations during fieldwork is through making written textual field notes. These can be augmented by other methods of recording – for example, photography, audio and video recording – but field notes remain a key part of ethnographic practice (Emerson et al., 2011; Sanjek, 1990; see also Banks, 2017; Gibbs, 2017). Field notes distinguish ethnographic observation from our everyday observations that we all undertake routinely in order to 'do' and make sense of our everyday lives. Participant observation generates field notes as data. Field notes provide a way of systematizing and recording our observations. During fieldwork the notes we are often able to make might be more jotting-like than lengthy field notes. It rather depends on the setting itself and the role the researcher adopts as to how easy, or otherwise, it is to write as you go – in the field. This is one reason why it is often helpful or indeed essential to ensure there are regular breaks or intervals between periods of observation, to ensure notes can be expanded and detailed, in ways that render them useful data. Notes in the field need to act as aide memoires, to prompt the transformation of our observations into rich and detailed description, as soon after the observation as is possible. Field notes are written compositions that are worked on and worked with; they are textual representations of the field, crafted and made by the ethnographer, drawing on literary conventions to produce thick description (Geertz, 1973), situating actions and interactions in contexts that render them meaningful to those not familiar with the setting.

Developing a well-organized and structured approach to the generation of field notes will stand you in good stead over the course of a research project. There are no rules as to how field notes should be constructed, for what to include and what not to. However, it is helpful to think about field notes providing detail that takes the reader 'there', such that they can visualize through a picture being painted with words. Field notes might typically include:

- A detailed description of the setting, including the materiality of the setting.
- Descriptions of people in the setting, using language that does not use judgements but rather describes what is seen.
- Timelines and chronologies of actions and events; what happened when, where and how.
- Descriptions of actions, interactions, behaviours and events, focusing on what is observable, not on perceptions or interpretations.
- Details of conversation, talk and other kinds of interaction, verbal (in full, verbatim where possible) as well as non-verbal.

There are also practical and organizational ways in which we can ensure that field notes are as good as they can be, and are as useful a source of ethnographic data as is possible. For example, ensuring field notes are well organized and clearly labelled with information about when and where the observation took place; recording data in sequence, chronologically where possible, so that actions and interactions can be reconstructed and 'remembered'; working at field notes that are richly descriptive of people, places and things, without recourse (at field note stage) to analysis or interpretation. Field notes should not include what we think is going on, only what we can see, hear and otherwise experience through our senses.

Field notes are texts that are produced (crafted) by the researcher as author, and in that, they can only ever be a textual representation of the field. While field notes should be carefully and thoughtfully written to provide vivid and rich descriptive accounts of the field, it is important to acknowledge their production as texts of the field. Ottenberg (1990) usefully coined the term 'head notes' to differentiate between field notes as a written record of fieldwork, and the tacit knowledge we come to know without even knowing (or being able to articulate that we know). However careful we are in writing up our notes of the field, there will remain things that we will remember and re-remember, things we come to know about in and of the field which escape a written form, but will inform, frame and enable reassessments of our interpretations and analyses over time. The ways we read and treat our field notes will change as our theoretical and methodological thinking matures, but the notes themselves will stay the same, written down as things happened and set in time. Head notes, though, are more dynamic and fluid, with the capacity to change after fieldwork as they did during fieldwork. Field notes are always themselves an aide memoire that are read and re-read by the ethnographer in conjunction with their experience of 'being there', and in relation to their thinking that will change through time and experience. Ottenberg (1990) suggests that it is precisely this relational interaction between field notes and head notes that 'makes' ethnography.

Participant observation, and the field notes that are integral to that approach, is an important part of ethnography. There has been long-standing debate as to how participant observation sits alongside other methods for ethnographic data collection, particularly interviewing (Becker and Geer, 1957a, 1957b; see also Atkinson et al., 2003, for an overview). The distinction is not quite so starkly drawn as we might imagine. Participant observation will usually involve opportunities or imperatives to speak to and ask questions of social actors in the setting.

ETHNOGRAPHIC CONVERSATIONS

In order to make sense of why things happen the way they do in social settings it is important, essential even, that we ask those who (may) know. During fieldwork, therefore, it is helpful and important that we engage in various kinds of conversation with social actors in and of the field. This can vary from what might appear to be the most casual of exchanges to much more formal, organized and structured interactions. We can use interviews, of various kinds and with varying degrees of organization and structure, to elicit member understandings of settings as part of ethnography. Burgess (1984, p. 102) coined the term 'conversation with a purpose' to describe ethnographic interviews as conversational interactions grounded in specific contexts and used to illustrate and exemplify what is being studied. This indicates that such interviews draw on conversational sensibilities and rules, are mutual interactions between researcher and informant and are encouraging of talk. That is, they are purposive in facilitating social actors in the field to describe phenomena that are part of their everyday worlds. The intention of interviews in ethnography, whether they occur in situ or by chance through everyday conversation during fieldwork, or through more planned and arranged opportunities, remains the same; that is, to gather information from people about their own experiences and understandings of the social setting.

Conversation and talk (see also Rapley, 2018) are part of our everyday worlds. We all engage in conversation as part of our everyday lives, though we rarely do so self-consciously. Talk does not just happen, however. There are conventions and rules that come into play in our conversational encounters, and these will differ depending on the situational context and the social actors involved. Indeed the very nature of conversations themselves can form the subject of detailed analysis; conversation analysis (ten Have, 2007) – the nuanced and situated study of social interaction, of 'talk' that might include both spoken and non-verbal 'speech' – is a sub-field of qualitative research and analysis in its own right. As part of ethnography fieldwork we may have the opportunity to record, verbatim, naturally occurring conversations and these can be subject to conversation analysis. Ethnographic interviews, however, are not 'naturally occurring'; they build on our conversational repertoire, but are interactions we are engaging in self-consciously and with purpose. We are deliberately entering into conversation in order to elicit accounts. The researcher is responsible for guiding the conversation, while at the same time ensuring that our informants have the opportunity to tell their stories in their own words and at their own pace. Of course, it is possible to collect accounts without deliberately seeking them out through explicitly questioning our informants. During fieldwork we may well be party to conversations that can provide rich information about views and perspectives in the field. It is also the case that informants will often share their accounts with us, particularly where rapport has been or is in the process of being established, with little prompting. During early stages of fieldwork, for example, people are often keen to make sure the researcher 'understands' what is going on. Of course, it is important to remain mindful that all accounts are situated within specific contexts and are from particular positions.

In social science research, a distinction is often made between structured and unstructured interviewing, with ethnographic interviewing often classified as being 'unstructured'. This is not necessarily a helpful distinction to make. All research interviews are, to an extent, structured events; they are interactional encounters between a researcher and an informant, at the very least structured by conversational norms and rules. The difference between ethnographic, qualitative interviews and other kinds of interviews (for example, survey interviews) is more in relation to the kinds of questions being asked, how those questions are posed and the ways in which the interview is structured as conversation. Ethnographic interviews are focused and purposive, but also dynamic and flexible. While the ethnographer may have areas of focus in mind, it is not necessary to know beforehand the precise questions that will be asked and in what ways. In fact, questions and topics for exploration may well emerge during an interview or interactional encounter, as the researcher *listens* to and responds to what is being said. This is a particularly important aspect of interviewing in ethnographic work. The interview is dialogic and fluid, albeit within the framework of a research agenda that has been set by the focus of the ethnographic inquiry. There will be times when the interview moves away from the agreed focus, perhaps when the informant answers a question in such a way that prompts new and different questions, or a new topic for discussion. This can be very productive and surprising, leading the research into areas that had not been anticipated. The skill of the researcher in such instances is to be able to tread a careful path between keeping an interview 'on track' and recognizing and exploring new lines of inquiry. It is the listening that is, then, vital to the ethnographic enterprise. And this means really listening and following up, not moving through a series of questions at speed and with an agenda that does not take account of what is being said and heard.

When undertaking interviews in ethnography, there is not always or often a fixed set of questions that we must stick to rigidly; it is more usual and appropriate to have an idea of the kinds of issues that you want to cover during the conversation; of areas where members' perspectives and experiences are of particular importance, if understanding of the setting is to be developed. Where such conversations occur in situ, as part of observational fieldwork and without prior planning, then the topics for discussion may well relate to what is going on 'right now', or what has happened 'just then'. Here the questioning might be subtle and immediate, providing an opportunity to follow up on events, behaviours and interactions that have been in some way observed and shared by the ethnographer and others in the field. Where there is the opportunity to plan the interview a little more, or where the primary method of data generation is to be interviews, thinking of the kinds of topics to be covered and questions to be asked is important. It is helpful to develop an aide memoire of topics and areas of focus, to structure the conversation. This can also be a useful thing to share with informants, so that they are clear about what you are interested in from the outset. It is also possible to co-produce the interview schedule, working with informants on agreeing topic areas that are of mutual interest, further enabling ethnographic understanding to be developed through the perspectives of those social actors who are participants in the setting. Interviews should not be designed to trip people up or catch people out; rather they provide interactional opportunities to gain member perspectives and views, in the context of the focus of the study.

Ethnographic interviews are often referred to as in-depth or deep interviews, indicating that they provide opportunities for the generation of rich, qualitative data. This means adopting styles of questioning which invite and prompt detailed description and accounts. Questions should be open-ended, and the interviewing style should be flexible and dynamic. There are a range of questioning styles and frames that can be used to encourage member accounts. Spradley (1979) provided a very useful framework for ethnographic interviewing; and one that continues to have relevance. Spradley describes a range of different kinds of question styles – for example, 'grand tour' questions which are opening non-directional invitations to an informant, general questions and the potentially wide ranging: 'Tell me about how things happen here', 'Can you describe what goes in this place?'. Such invitations give permission for informants to start their description at a point and in a way that is relevant to them. 'Mini-tour' questions might be used to follow up, by asking for more detail on a particular aspect of experience or activity alluded to or already mentioned by the informant. Further, there are questions that can be used to extend and probe, providing opportunities to add layers of detail – questions that ask for instances and examples to illustrate a point perhaps, contrast questions which invite comparison, clarification questions which can be used to confirm meaning and so on. Depending on where the interview is taking place and/or the resources to hand, informants can also be asked to 'show' as well as 'tell'– either through walking through or showing the researcher something in situ in the setting, or by recreating or reconstructing events, activities or experiences through diagrams, drawings or in some other medium.

As well as questioning styles there are other factors to take into consideration when conducting ethnographic interviews. While it is important to avoid leading questions that suggest a judgement, moral or otherwise, on what is being told to you, directional questions can be useful to prompt further elicitation on a particular point. While the overarching structure of an ethnographic interview should be non-directive, listening to and questioning in response to what is being said is important, and in that context specific and highly focused directional questions can be used to test out our understanding. Directional questions should be used with care, and asked with an awareness of the likely effect of the question on the answers that are forthcoming. Similarly, it is important to follow up on new topics and issues that are introduced by the informant over the course of the conversation;

not just press on with the set of questions you had in mind regardless of the new lines of inquiry or ways of seeing that present themselves. Of course if you feel the informant has gone way off track, shifting the conversation back to the general area of focus is a particularly valuable skill.

Interviews, as with conversations, have verbal and non-verbal aspects. While it is important that the researcher does not dominate the conversation, nor should they be passive. The usual etiquette of conversations should be observed. For example, maintaining eye contact, and giving both verbal and non-verbal cues to indicate 'you understand', or that what is being said is of interest to you (for instance, smiling, nodding your head, utterances that indicate active listening is taking place). It is equally important to think through the local context of the interview. For example, choosing an appropriate location in which to undertake the interview where informants will feel comfortable and safe, and perhaps where they will have some control over the interview encounter, for instance by offering refreshments or otherwise hosting you. Similarly it is courteous to negotiate a time that fits in with the schedule and life of informants, being sensitive to their constraints. We should also be mindful that interviews are a means to access and generate data, and hence those data need to be recorded in some way. Where possible audio recording is helpful, but depending on where you are interviewing and who you are interviewing that might not be possible or desirable. Interviews that spontaneously occur during participant observation might be particularly difficult to audio record. Conversations might take place 'on the move' and in places replete with sounds of the everyday. Noisy places cannot always be avoided, nor should they be necessarily, though this might create challenges for how to capture data in ways that are easily retrievable (see Hall et al., 2008, for a discussion of sounds in fieldwork). Where audio recording is possible, additional permissions should always be sought and the decision of the informant in this regard respected. Without recourse to any kind of recording device the ethnographer relies on taking field notes to capture interview conversation, trying to ensure that notes are as detailed and as verbatim as possible. In fact even where interview conversations are being digitally recorded, notes can serve a useful purpose. Note-taking provides an opportunity for natural pauses in conversation, which might be helpful to both parties. Notes also enable non-verbal information about the interview to be recorded and provide a strategy for making sure we listen. There is a tendency when things are being technologically recorded that we stop actively listening; this is particularly unhelpful in ethnographic, qualitative interviews where we want to follow up on topics and lines of inquiry that are being offered by our informants.

Ethnographic interviews – whether formally orchestrated meetings or more spontaneous conversations during fieldwork – are useful in relation to the spoken data that are gathered during the encounter. What is said and how it is said can provide useful lines for analysis (see Chapter 6 on analyzing narratives). Interviews can also be viewed as opportunities for participant observation. The interview encounter can provide important insights into how social actors present themselves. There are some interesting points of comparison here between participant observation and interviewing. They are not so very different, and both have a place in ethnography. Both are concerned with exploring the performance of social action. There have been long-standing debates within ethnography as to whether more authentic data collection comes with participant observation and whether the interview is in some ways a more artificial medium through which accounts are, perhaps, more purposively contrived. And indeed whether interviews are less 'natural' and thus more susceptible to researcher bias. This does an injustice to interviewing in the context of ethnographic work, as well as misrepresenting participant observation. Participant observation is similarly interactional and relational. Ethnographic interviews draw on what social actors do every day to perform social actions and 'do' social life. They can be appropriate ways of eliciting not only accounts of experience but also the performance of social action. Interviews can be analyzed in relation to the information that is being shared, but can also be interrogated in relation to the cultural resources informants use to construct and tell their accounts, as well as the functions that may be enacted through these culturally mediated ways of telling. Heyl (2001, p. 370) notes that ethnographic interviewing occupies something of a middle place 'surrounded by debates about what can be known (for example, can scientific methods access the real world?) and challenged by issues raised by poststructuralist, feminist and multicultural scholars'. Nevertheless, she notes agreement on some of the underlying goals of interviewing as part of ethnography: 'listening well and respectfully', acquiring 'a self-awareness of our role in the co-construction of meaning', being 'cognizant of ways in which both the ongoing relationship and the broader social context affect the participants [and] the interview process', and 'recognizing that dialogue is discovery and only partial knowledge will ever be attained'.

DOCUMENTARY REALITIES OF SOCIAL LIFE

Most ethnographic research takes place in settings that are 'documented' in some shape or form. Most social settings are self-documenting, and therefore we can draw on archival and documentary materials as part of ethnographic work. What is meant by documents (see also Rapley, 2018) can be very broad. Most settings will generate 'official' or administrative records of various kinds. There are also various everyday documents of organizations that can be important ways in which social life is enacted and understood – for example, minutes of meetings, notes, reports and case records. Surveys might be routinely undertaken in a setting and data published. Documents of life (Plummer, 2001) can also include diaries, biographical testimony, maps, photographs and newspaper reports; these are physical traces of settings and of lives. Such documents can also be viewed as primary sources of data for the ethnographer. As well as being useful ways of familiarizing ourselves with a setting prior to fieldwork, the collecting and analyzing of documents can also form part of our ethnographic practice. So, for example, it might be possible to collect existing photographs or generate new photographs as part of an ethnographic project. Of course, documents are not just written texts, social worlds are also documented and displayed through a range of visual materials that construct and present the social world in pictures as well as words. The analysis of visual materials has been a growing field of scholarly activity within qualitative social science (Stanczak, 2007; Banks and Zeitlyn, 2015; see also Banks, 2018). Rose (2007) refers to the social life of images, capturing anthropological and ethnographic interest in visual materials as part of the way in which social and cultural life endures. Attending to the visual has increasingly been seen as part of the ways in which knowledge can be produced in ethnography (Pink, 2007). Serious consideration should be given to the ways in which visual materials might be collected and generated within an ethnographic project, mindful of how such data will be analytically treated. As Pink (2007, p. 19) acknowledges, visual methods in ethnography 'may unexpectedly become part of an ethnographic project that is already in progress' or can be planned in from the beginning as part of the research design. This relates both to visual materials that might already exist in and of a field, and to visual data that might be made during fieldwork by the ethnographer, by our informants or through co-production.

There are also many digital documentary traces of contemporary social life; for example, email conversations, SMS text messaging, websites, social media and **hypermedia** environments. Increasingly these offer multimodal documentary realities, often incorporating a range of modes and media including text, image and sound. Multimedia, of course, offers possibilities for the ethnographer, both for the ways in which observations are recorded by the researcher and in relation to the media that can be collected by the researcher during fieldwork (Dicks et al., 2005). Virtual environments and digital forms of data, increasingly routinely generated as part of everyday cultural life, also serve to expand and challenge the ethnographic repertoire in relation to data collection *and* analysis. Interviews and observations can be conducted in and through virtual worlds and media; interactions that are screen-mediated generate different forms of data, with different linguistic and interactional qualities; readily available technological resources stretch the possibilities of what counts as data and how data might be recorded in ethnography.

To return to the more general point, of which technological capacity and capability is one part, all kinds of documents are routinely written, produced, read, consumed, stored, circulated and used in social and cultural life. There may also be secondary data sources that can be used to inform our ethnographic research. For example, novels can be a useful way of contextualizing a setting; and earlier studies of the setting or of similar settings may have produced written accounts that can be read to inform new data collection. Increasingly researchers are also archiving their data for other researchers to use through secondary analysis; indeed there are interesting debates and tensions in relation to the ways in which ethnographers can and should share data, particularly in the context of the creation and authorship of field notes and the presence of the researcher (Hammersley, 2009). But existing ethnographic data that are available become documents of the field, physical traces that can be explored in relation to ongoing and new ethnographic inquiry.

May (2001, p. 176) provides an evocative justification for including documents in our ethnographic research practice, as part of our fieldwork – 'documents, read as the sedimentations of social practices, have the potential to inform and structure the decisions which people make on a daily and longer-term basis: they also constitute particular readings of social events'. Ethnographic study can benefit from a careful and critical attention to the gathering and analysis of documents, of various kinds, in various modes and through various media. Documents contain socially (and perhaps also technologically) mediated information about a setting. Appreciating how documents function in a setting, and are produced, authored, composed, shared, received and circulated, can enhance our understanding of social life and social practice.

Documents can be a rich resource for the ethnographer, though utilizing or generating documentary data is not without its challenges. Documents may not of course be readily available; co-producing visual or other materials may not be appropriate or possible. It is also important to recognize that documentary materials will have been authored using particular literary conventions, or in relation to particular forms of artistic practice. They will have been produced with particular purposes in mind. In that sense, it is important that documents are not viewed as providing some kind of documented 'truth' about a setting. Rather documents of social life must be understood and analyzed for what they are and what they might tell us about the settings we seek to understand. Documents, in all their forms, modes and media are socially produced 'accounts' of various kinds, re-presenting settings, organizations and lives in particular kinds of ways and for particular kinds of reasons. This is precisely why they are valuable ethnographic resources.

KEY POINTS

- Ethnographic data are generated by the researcher's engagement with and interactions in the field. In that sense data are co-productions by the researcher and the field of study.
- Principal data collection techniques used in ethnographic fieldwork are participant observation and in-depth interviews.
- Data collection begins from the moment the ethnographer encounters the research setting. First days in the field can generate significant data and challenge our preconceptions.
- The participant observer is not a neutral or objective position. The ethnographer brings with them their experiences, assumptions and personal characteristics. These should be points for reflection and constructive challenge.
- Ethnographic interviews can usefully be described as purposeful conversations. They are dialogic and dynamic in nature.
- Questioning styles in ethnographic interviewing are open but focused, and are used to elicit member accounts.
- Documents form part of social and cultural life. They can be collected or generated alongside other data as part of ethnography.
- The documentary realities of social life can include written, visual and multimodal materials, including digital and new forms of data.

FURTHER READING

Delamont, S. (2002) *Fieldwork in Educational Settings*, 2nd ed. London and New York: Routledge.

Emerson, R.M., Fretz, R.I. and Shaw, L.L. (2011) *Writing Ethnographic Fieldnotes*, 2nd ed. Chicago: University of Chicago Press.

Heyl, B.S. (2001) 'Ethnographic interviewing', in P. Atkinson, A. Coffey, S. Delamont, J. Lofland and L. Lofland (eds), *Handbook of Ethnography*. London: Sage, pp. 369–84.

FIELD ROLES AND RELATIONSHIPS

CONTENTS

After reading this chapter, you will:

- appreciate the ways in which researcher characteristics, identities and experiences impact upon the possibilities of ethnographic fieldwork;
- know about some of the roles that ethnographers can adopt in the field and during fieldwork; and
- further understand the ways in which ethnographic fieldwork is personal and relational.

THE RESEARCHER AND THE FIELD

Ethnographic research requires the researcher to be engaged and present. Indeed the most important tool in and of ethnography is the researcher. The ethnographer must put themselves into a position where they can participate in a setting, and interact with people within that setting, in order to develop knowledge, document, represent and come to understand. In the social anthropological tradition of ethnography, research was and can be a prolonged and deep engagement of a researcher with a field of inquiry; an act of immersion that may take place over months, years, decades or a lifetime. For some ethnographers the relationship with a setting develops over multiple return visits and can span a whole career (Fowler and Hardesty, 1994; Okely and Callaway, 1992). Ethnography, in this sense, might constitute a life's work, and that life – the researcher's life – might well be fundamentally shaped by and intertwined with the setting and the relationships which are formed with participants. Of course, contemporary ethnographic practice is more varied and diverse than this scenario. Over the course of a career a researcher might undertake a number of ethnographic studies in a range of settings. The adoption of ethnographic methods across the social science and humanities disciplines, and within modern-day research work contexts that cannot necessarily support the kind of prolonged engagement articulated by the anthropological imperative, has changed the ways in which the contemporary ethnographer is situated within the field. Periods of participant observation might be relatively short, certainly rarely spanning years or longer, and might be just long enough to glean useful insight and understanding. And where time is short, there might be more reliance on conversation – on ethnographic interviews – than necessarily on lengthy observational fieldwork. Interviews can seem, at first glance at least, more manageable, time efficient and easier to schedule, than 'hanging out' in a setting for long periods of time. However, the positionality of the researcher is no less significant in these seemingly more bounded and less wide-ranging ethnographic encounters. The ethnographer remains key to these, perhaps more modest, ethnographic endeavours. Who we are, what we bring to our fieldwork and indeed what we become over the course of our research, defines and shapes the data we produce in the field and how we come to make sense of those data through our analyses and writing.

In this chapter the roles and relationships of fieldwork are explored. This includes consideration of what we bring with us when we undertake research – how our own characteristics, experiences and positionalities impact upon the possibilities of fieldwork. The chapter also explores the roles that we can and do adopt during fieldwork, how those can change over time and in different contexts, as well as the relationships that are formed and developed during our research.

WHAT WE BRING TO FIELDWORK

Ethnographic research positions the researcher within the research setting, and hence we need to be mindful of how we fit in with or impact upon the field of study. We might usefully think of this in two ways. Firstly, in relation to what we bring to a setting – those personal characteristics, experiences and ideas that might prove to be useful or problematic to fieldwork; that we might choose to emphasize or may need to sensitively manage, as we access a setting and go about developing productive fieldwork relations. The second way in which we can consider the positionality of the researcher is in relation to the shaping of our experiences during fieldwork; how our own relations of ethnographic practice structure our fieldwork experiences and sense of self.

Accessing a setting means giving careful consideration to the ways in which we manage our presentation of self. Impression management, thinking about our self-presentation in relation to the setting we are seeking access to study, is important. This might include taking very practical steps; for example, taking care of how we dress – perhaps to mirror those we are studying, or lessen the difference – but also thinking about our styles of everyday interaction and how these might need to be modified in the field. For instance, while it is not always necessary to take on the appearance or speech codes of social actors in our field of study, it is important to be mindful of, and sensitive to, how we might appear or come across within a setting. It is helpful and appropriate to be sensitive to the cultural codes and norms of the setting. Of course, in order to 'impression manage', we need to know something about the setting and the people we are planning to work with. Part of our initial fieldwork and scoping can usefully focus on the ways in which people present in the setting, and therefore what might be an appropriate stance for the researcher to adopt. So, for example, the ways in which we might dress and present ourselves will be different if we are undertaking research in a youth club setting or in an international accountancy firm. I have undertaken research in both settings. While in both cases I was undertaking overt research (it was known and accepted that I was a researcher), it was important that I indicated through my appearance and manner that I understood the ways in which the settings operated. While I was not aspiring to be a full participant, it was sensitive and appropriate to those settings that I fitted in. In the accountancy firm, I adopted a code of dress and appearance similar to the graduate accountants I was engaging with – a business suit, smart shoes, long coat and briefcase. In the youth club settings where I have also undertaken research I have modified my appearance in different ways, including adopting a more casual mode of dress, which I deemed was more appropriate to those settings. In both instances, the aim was to not appear too different in the context of the research setting, and to be respectful of the perceived norms of appearance. However, such aspirations were tempered by what was possible, given my personal characteristics and resources to hand. When I was undertaking ethnographic fieldwork in an accountancy firm, I was near to the age of and had similar educational experiences to the graduate accountants. I was not so very far from their life worlds. I could easily have chosen the career path they had embarked on. It was possible for me to blend in during training courses and on visits to clients. Adopting a similar style of dress was relatively easy, and was part of a more general set of considerations as to how I drew on my own experiences and characteristics to establish rapport and my own role within the field. This had to be differently approached in the case of youth club settings. I was nearer the age of the youth workers than the young people. My experiences and life worlds were closer to those of the workers than of the young people. It was not appropriate, desirable or really possible for me to 'dress like the kids'; I could not pass as a teenager, but by looking 'like' the youth workers I was able to situate myself sensitively within the settings. This, of course, raises other issues about the possibilities of fieldwork in relation to who we are and where we are coming from – for example, it is possible to undertake ethnographic fieldwork in youth work settings without being a young person, but it is not possible to be a full participant observer as a teenager unless you are a teenager. The appearances we can craft, the roles we can adopt and the fieldwork relations we are able to establish are all mediated by our own sense of self. Of course, managing self during fieldwork is not just about the practicalities of dress or other explicit markers of appearance. We also bring to the field various personal characteristics and identities that it may not be possible to change, but that nevertheless may need to be managed or otherwise acknowledged during fieldwork. For example, our perceived gender, age and ethnicity, among other factors, may impact upon the roles it is possible to adopt and the relationships it is possible to form in the field. Indeed, there might be some settings where our own personal characteristics might limit what is possible, or will make accessing some settings or some people difficult. In many cases, researchers are able to navigate their personal characteristics and markers of identity in relation to the study setting. It is rarely the case that who we are makes fieldwork impossible. However, there may well be imperatives to think critically and creatively in relation to both how to present oneself in and to a setting (including to different groups within a setting), and how we can and do make sense of a setting from our particular positionalities. For instance, women researchers have reflected upon their status and the impact of gender on fieldwork relations. For example, Hutheesing's single status was an issue during fieldwork in northern Thailand, where her informants tried to 'marry her off', albeit good naturedly (1993). Abu-Lughod (1988) recounted her experience of conducting research in a Bedouin culture where young, single women living alone were seen as problematic. She countered this by always conforming to what she deemed to be appropriate and modest forms of dress, and by being especially careful about how she described her home life to her hosts in the field, letting them believe that she lived near to her father; an unmarried women living on her own was considered odd and dangerous. The presence or absence of children has also been reflected upon in relation to understanding fieldwork dynamics. Berik (1996) was the recipient of concern during her research in rural Turkey due to her perceived childlessness. After finding out she was married, but without children, informants would offer consolation, and her field relations were, in part at least, managed in relation to this perceived sadness in her life.

It would be easy to conclude that it is only during extended fieldwork in cultures that are anthropologically strange that our personal lives have the capacity to impact on field relations. This would be to miss the general point – in all ethnographic research our personal selves are present. Understanding how we will be perceived in the field, managing who we are, within those very limits of who we are, is essential to productive and reflective fieldwork. The value of thinking through and addressing our own personal characteristics and markers of identity in the context of the fieldwork encounter takes us beyond the personal, of course. There is ethnographic value in recognizing and working within and in relation to the personal frames of reference of the settings we are seeking to understand. For example, the 'perceived' gendered structures of a setting can take on particularly transparent meaning when you are experiencing them first hand, and they are being mediated through your own experiences. Equally, developing an awareness of how our own age, personal status, sexuality or ethnicity (and so on) is impacting upon or has the capacity to impact upon field relations becomes part of the way in which we come to understand a setting. Our own identity work, of who we are and how that is revealed and managed in the context of fieldwork, is an important part of the ethnographic encounter, and is an important mechanism through which we can gain an understanding of the setting under investigation.

This identity work extends to the roles, knowledges and experiences we bring to the field, and how we might utilize these for ethnographic purpose. Fieldwork is not always conducted by those who are 'strangers' to a particular setting. Indeed it is not so unusual for researchers to bring substantial prior knowledge and understanding with them to the field. Of course, in the case of prolonged fieldwork, including where there might be many returns to the setting, the ethnographer may also increasingly become a knowledgeable 'insider' over time. Social anthropologists have reflected on their changing understandings, roles and relationships within a setting in and through time, often encompassing years or decades of ethnographic research (Fowler and Hardesty, 1994). There are also many examples of ethnography conducted 'at home', in settings that are familiar, and where fieldwork is undertaken from an assumed position of knowing, for instance in the case of ethnographies of occupational settings undertaken by members or ex-members of those occupations. For example, there are ethnographic studies of nursing and midwifery by practitioners in and of the field (e.g. see, Davies, 1994; Hunt, 1987); of military life by former members of the armed forces (Hockey, 1986, 1996); of policing and prisons undertaken by ex-police-officers (Carter, 1994); of social work settings conducted by social workers (Pithouse, 1987; Scourfield, 2003); and school-based ethnographies conducted by former school teachers (Ball, 1981; Burgess, 1983; Pollard, 1985).

Familiarization and immersion (or conversion) raise particular opportunities and challenges for ethnography. There are well-established debates within ethnography in relation to familiarity and strangeness, and the relative merits and problems of being too close to those settings being studied (see Atkinson et al., 2003, for a summary). For our purposes here, a main message is that we bring to our research identities, roles, knowledges and experiences that structure and frame our research encounters; who we are impacts upon our choices of research setting (see Chapter 3, this volume), the relationships it is possible to develop during our research, as well as the ways in which we understand and articulate what is happening in the field. What we bring to our research in terms of our sense of self must be reflected on from the outset, prior to as well as during and after fieldwork. The ways in which the self is defined, how we locate ourselves in relation to a field of study, and being reflexive about the self are important parts of, rather than tangential to, ethnographic research practice. A reality of ethnography is the active involvement of the researcher in the setting under study, and the possibilities of relationships that ethnographers forge in the field. There has been a long-standing concern with the dangers of immersion or over-familiarity in ethnography. It has been argued that too much familiarity can lead to an inability to 'see', with attendant risks of taking activities and interactions for granted rather than subjecting them to analytical attention. More productively, perhaps, it is important to guard against a failure to acknowledge who we are, and how who we are impacts upon the realities and possibilities of fieldwork. This demands that the ethnographer is a reflexive practitioner.

ROLES IN THE FIELD

All ethnographic research involves the researcher having some role or another during the research. A classic typology of roles adopted by researchers in the field was outlined by Gold (1958), and still has contemporary relevance (see also Junker, 1960). Gold outlined a continuum of roles, with different degrees of participation and observation. This continuum included;

- *The complete observer:* where the researcher is detached from the setting, perhaps not even seen or noticed, with little appetite, deemed necessity or opportunity for participation. The complete observer role is predicated on an assumption that the researcher does not interact with the field or with participants. Such a position is actually quite hard to reconcile with ethnographic research practice, and is certainly very difficult to maintain in the field. It is hard to be and to remain invisible.
- *The observer as participant:* where the researcher is identified within the setting and relates to people in the setting, but very clearly only as a researcher. Here, the researcher remains peripheral to the actions and events within that setting, and will have limited levels of participation, through choice or opportunity. Their presence is acknowledged as a researcher.
- *The participant as observer:* where the researcher is engaged within the setting, actively participating in activities and interactions as opportunities are presented or made. Here, the researcher navigates a role between participant and observer, maintaining a researcher status while becoming part of the setting.
- *The complete participant:* where the researcher becomes or is a full member of the setting, fully engaged and participant in the everyday world of that setting; and where the role of researcher is perhaps indistinguishable from that of participant.

If these roles can be considered as falling along a continuum, most ethnographers would adopt a role somewhere around the middle. There may well be, in any ethnographic project, occasions where assuming a role as a complete observer or a complete participant is necessary or appropriate. For example, at the start of a project it may be difficult or impossible to participate in any way at all, and the stance of the outside observer may be the best or most appropriate role. Equally, particularly in prolonged fieldwork, or where research is being conducted in a setting in which we are already an integral part, there might be times when participation is full, and the observer role is temporarily forgotten or arrested by both the research and the research participants. Of course, there might be aspects of a setting where any kind of participation on the part of the researcher might be difficult or dangerous or risky. For example, if you are undertaking an ethnography of a hospital setting it may be the case that you are only permitted to 'watch' an operating theatre from the position of complete observer, not interacting or engaging at all with the activities and interactions of that setting. You may only be able to experience that particular event from a distance. Covert research can also bring with it the imperative of adopting the role of complete participant in order to access and observe a particular setting. The roles of complete observer or complete participant can bring with them particular ethical issues that might need to be addressed, as well as methodological challenges. A complete observer implies a passivity that might prevent the opportunity of gaining member understandings of settings. Equally, complete participation can mean that we start to take things for granted and 'not see' what there is to be seen.

There are other ways in which to conceptualize the ethnographer role or terms of engagement with the field. Adler and Adler (1994) used the term 'membership' to describe the ways in which ethnographer roles are framed; hence we might think of researchers who are:

- complete members;
- active members;
- marginal or peripheral members.

Complete members fully participate in the setting, and in so doing share values, understandings and experiences. Active members are able and willing to join in readily with activities, events and interactions, while maintaining a distinct researcher role. Marginal or peripheral membership implies just that – while the researcher develops a relationship with people in the setting and establishes an acceptable identity in the field, they participate infrequently or not at all in everyday core activities and events.

These roles of 'membership' serve to remind us that there are strategic and pragmatic decisions in relation to the possibilities of participation in ethnographic fieldwork. Of course, how a role is developed during fieldwork is a little more complex than simply choosing a suitable or preferable persona. Our roles in the field might be, and often are, multiple, fluid and subject to change – over time, in different contexts and with different people in the setting. In my own ethnographic research with an international accountancy firm, I had given little thought to the role or roles I would adopt prior to beginning fieldwork, short of appreciating a general imperative to establish rapport and to be respectful of the setting under study. While the organizational setting I was studying was analytically and experientially 'strange' to me, I was also researching reasonably 'close to home', within a relatively local organization and with people whom I had perceived were not too distant from my own sense of self. I was familiar with the 'kind of people' in the setting. The graduate accountants at the heart of my study were of a similar age to me. Indeed I had debated with myself as to whether I should train as an accountant following my degree studies (in fact I trained as a school teacher). I had friends who were accountants, and I had assumed, in so far as I had thought about it at all, that I would have little difficulty combining my 'in the field' and 'out of the field' senses of self. And yet the realities of fieldwork led me towards developing and adopting a number of roles in the field, all of them authentic, but not always complementary to one another. I was able to establish good relationships with most of the graduate accountants in the organization from the outset. However, while courteous and respectful to all of my research participants, I found myself 'naturally' drawn to some more than others, and them to me. For some I remained a researcher and they the participants of my study. We had a mutual understanding that I was doing a job and was interested in their working lives. With others, I developed friendships in the field, meeting them outside of the 'work' setting, partly to follow up on events that had happened during fieldwork, but also sharing social time and, in time, confidences. I also participated in the training encounters of the graduate trainees, and in that sense became a fellow student. I found myself genuinely worrying about whether I was grasping the material that was being taught in training sessions. While I knew, and my fellow students knew, I was not actually training to be an accountant, the anxiety I felt in relation to some of the accountancy tasks 'we' were set was real, or at least it felt so at the time. Later in the fieldwork, as my rapport developed with the training tutor, and following a planned ethnographic interview, we began to discuss our shared experience of teaching – my role as a 'fellow teacher' was helpful in both establishing rapport and gaining insight into the ways in which graduate accountants were being trained. Equally, to access the high echelons of the organization, the role I adopted navigated a pathway between an assumed naïvety (showing a willingness to learn and wanting to be genuinely informed by those more knowledgeable than me as to how the organization worked) and that of a fellow professional from a cognate organization. So, over the course of the fieldwork I actually adopted a range of variously participant roles. Some were very self-consciously chosen by me, some were chosen for me by participants, while others emerged more 'naturally' through shared understandings, experiences and developing personal friendships. I was, among other roles, teacher, friend, researcher, fellow student, lecturer, confidante and fellow professional. All of these roles were mediated by an identity in the field as a pseudo graduate accountant – a participant in the accountancy world, without (quite) becoming an accountant. Moreover, I also recognized or came to recognize that all of the roles were framed within the ethnographic imperative; I remained a researcher accessing the field in order to study and in turn to write about a social world (Coffey, 1999).

The role of the naïve incompetent has particular purchase in ethnography. Such a role assumes a position of 'unknowing', of being unfamiliar with, or a stranger to, a setting. Such a stance can afford the researcher the opportunity to ask relatively naïve questions from a position of assumed ignorance, and places the emphasis on social actors in the field as knowledgeable. Such a position can assist with developing rapport and can mediate issues of power in the field, making it clear that it is participants who 'know' and are expert, and it is the ethnographer who is learning. The naïve incompetent is an entirely legitimate role to adopt, at least initially, though it may be hard to maintain in the longer term. It is simply not possible to keep claiming ignorance after prolonged engagement with the field, and indeed can be counterproductive. It is important that we demonstrate to our participants that our understanding of the field is developing as they share their perspectives and experiences with us. Equally, in some settings, where the ethnographer already has an obvious or declared understanding (perhaps due to some kind of insider status), it might be difficult to sustain such a role in the first place. The opposite position, of course, is an over-familiarization with a setting. It can be hard to claim ignorance in a setting with which you are or where you become extremely familiar. Moreover, new strategies for observation, and for conversation, might need to be adopted where familiarization starts to stop you 'seeing' and 'hearing'. The morality tale of over-familiarity in ethnography is a well-trodden path. There continues to be a widely held assumption that ethnographers should guard against total immersion in the field, and becoming a full member, for fear of a lack of analytical distance. Total role transformation is not supposed to happen during fieldwork. Over-identification has been held up as signalling doom and failure. Such a stance can also signal a lack of understanding of what can be highly complex and nuanced field relations. It is certainly the case that an over-identification without critical reflection may well lead to a particularly partial reading of a setting. But with self-awareness and good reflexivity this does not need to be the case. Moreover, we must recognize that all ethnographic research will necessarily only ever provide us with partial knowledge and understanding. The point with any role adopted or assumed in the field (however familiar and comfortable we become) is not to lose the analytical capacity to 'see', to 'hear', and to document, in order to develop understanding. It is appropriate to recognize that, in ethnography, we are and become part of what we study, that we are and will be affected by the specific contexts within which we are researching, and that we are shaped by our fieldwork experiences. It is epistemologically important to do so, and unhelpful to deny the self an active and situated place in the field. Pragmatically and intellectually, it is important, also, to recognize that the aim of ethnographic research is to develop understanding and come to make sense of social worlds. The roles we develop and adopt should be sympathetic with that imperative; but there are many possible roles and positions. It is worth remembering that most of us will intrude on a setting and on the lives of our participants for a relatively short length of time; not surprising therefore that the impact of fieldwork may often be greater for us than for our hosts. Our fieldwork experiences will almost definitely shape our lives more than those of our participants.

RELATIONSHIPS IN THE FIELD

Ethnographic fieldwork is relational. While research settings and experiences will differ greatly, they all share a common factor. Research settings and our ethnographic experiences of them are social and relational; fields are 'peopled' by social actors as well as the researcher. The ways in which we set about our research task, of data gathering in order to understand and make sense of social worlds, are framed by and through social interaction and shared experiences with others. Hence fieldwork is dependent upon, and shaped by, relationships established and developed over time and in place. Indeed, it is difficult to think about effective ethnographic fieldwork without paying attention to the relationships that make it so. In some ways such relationships are similar to all of our other relations of social life – perhaps built on mutual trust, common experiences or shared understandings, or by instrumental concerns. Equally, social relations of course are not always congenial or positive. Ethnographic field relationships mirror the complexity of our everyday relationships. Fieldwork relationships are at once personal and professional, and there is often much at stake in terms of research success. Many of our professional interactions, perhaps in the workplace, are built upon courtesy and polite acquaintance. But in ethnographic fieldwork such professional distance may well prove inadequate. Good, productive fieldwork relies on personal investment by the researcher in the relations of the field. Relationships in the field, in their many and varied guises, are real in their consequences – impacting on the quality of data and analyses and on the lived experience of ethnographic practice.

The onus of building rapport, and of establishing appropriate and meaningful relationships, is firmly upon the researcher in ethnographic work. In terms of our research agenda, these relationships matter particularly to us. That is not to deny that relationships are not or do not become meaningful to participants in the field. Navigating these professional, and what might become personal, relationships is a key feature of ethnographic work. Reciprocity, authenticity and genuineness are vexed issues for the ethnographer. Imbalances in personal commitment and invest-ment can lead to difficult, tense and potentially exploitative situations. Equally, the fact that the success of fieldwork might rely upon the quality of our personal relationships potentially places us at risk of vulnerability and hurt.

One particular aspect of the relations of fieldwork is the ways in which we develop our relationships with key informants in our research, and the complexi-ties of friendship in and beyond the field. Of course, fieldwork relationships with key social actors are situated within particular cultural and research contexts. While they might build on pre-existing relations, they are forged and consolidated during shared fieldwork experiences. There are many examples of where genu-ine mutual friendships have developed during ethnographic research, and indeed have then transcended the research encounter. However, it should be recognized that such friendships can be complicated. Crick (1992), for example, observed that such relations are inevitably ironic, where ethnographer and informant might conspire to create a working fiction of friendship, but where the reality is a shared falsehood. Crick drew on his own experience of his 'friendship' with Ali, a key informant during ethnographic fieldwork in Sri Lanka. Crick reflected that to call Ali a friend or an informant would be 'to say too much' and also to 'leave something important out' (1992, p. 177). Similarly, Hendry (1992) has described her relationship with Sachiko, who was a fellow student, then a friend, and later became a key informant and gatekeeper during ethnographic research in Japan. The two of them later worked together as research collaborators. Defining and understanding the boundaries and possibilities of friendship was epistemologi-cally important for Hendry, though also personally difficult, not least because the friendship eventually broke down.

My own experience of friendship in the field has also been both productive and problematic. My developing friendship with a key informant during my research in an international accountancy firm was highly productive in terms of my ethnographic research agenda. Our friendship developed in the context of my research project. We would not have met without the ethnography I was undertaking. Our friendship was predicated on our shared perspectives and interests; we began to meet socially 'outside' of the field setting, though for me it remained unclear as to whether those meetings were still being undertaken as part of the ethnography. I think we shared a working understanding that I was interested in her work, and she shared her experiences, and had numerous conversations with me about a wide range of topics, some not connected to her work at all. We discussed interests and our personal relationships. While I did not take detailed field notes during our social times together, I did find myself making jottings and notes to myself when I returned home from our evenings out, keen to remember insights and explanations that would aid my understanding of the field and provide ideas for further fieldwork. As fieldwork progressed I shared some of my field notes with my fieldwork friend, and tested out some of my emergent understandings of what was, in fact, her everyday world. For me, the friendship felt authentic, even though I was acutely mindful of the circumstances under which we had met. My memories of our shared times remain important to me, not just in terms of the ethnography but also in relation to my personal sense of self and what was going on in my life then. Who I was and became, alongside the capacity I had to undertake the research, was enhanced and underpinned by that friendship. It is, of course, impossible for me to know how she viewed our friendship. And, obviously, the friendship was predicated on and framed by my emergent and developing research agenda. As well as a friend, she was and remained my key informant. When we had personal disagreements, I know I was very conscious of my research imperative and was always quick to make amends or to move the conversation on (on reflection much quicker than I usually am, with even very good and very old friends). At the end of the research, and particular after I had left the field and written my ethnography (or should that be our ethnography?), the authenticity of the friendship was tested. From the positions of ethnographer and informant, we found that we disagreed over what had happened in the field, and in particular with my interpretation and analysis of some events. The imbalance of our friendship became stark and clear. I was writing about the work and life of my key informant, writing for an academic audience and not for her. My writing and analyses were of her experiences, but not for her, rather (perhaps) for me. It was my ethnography, in which she had a leading part. For both of us, the context of fieldwork had created, encouraged and in the end served to limit our friendship. If we were not bound by the relations of the field, perhaps I would have been more willing to challenge and argue, and to fight for our friendship on personal terms. Instead it seemed more appropriate and professional to agree to disagree. We had both, perhaps, imagined that the friendship stood outside of fieldwork, instead of being a key part of it. The ethnography was us and also stood in the way of us. While we had trust in each other, and shared intimate aspects of our lives, both of us came to understand too, the ways in which our friendship was contrived. The reciprocity of the friendship was based on our relative positions in and of the field; sustaining our friendship beyond the field was difficult because we could not, or perhaps would not reconcile our fieldwork selves and our other selves.

Ethnographic friendships are complex and complicated. They can and do exist, and it is important that they are acknowledged as part of the ethnographic act. They also serve to raise our awareness of some of the dichotomies of ethnographic practice – for example, how we reconcile or must work between the spaces of distance versus intimacy, or involvement versus detachment. Friendships in and of the field serve to draw attention to some of the tensions, as well as joys, of conducting ethnographic fieldwork and can be used to sharpen our abilities for critical reflection. They are also a useful point of departure in reminding us of the ways in which relationships are important to the ethnographic research act, and that such relationships need to be carefully considered and reflected upon, both in themselves and for the traces they leave behind. Throughout the ethnographic research process we are actively engaged in crafting and mediating selves in the context of personal relationships. Such relationships are also the vehicle through which we develop knowledge and understanding. Relations in and of the field are influenced and framed by those cultural norms and expectations that we bring as well as those we meet. It is the interactions between these two sets that become productive points of learning. It is precisely through the careful negotiation of social relations in the field that we can come to know the field that we are seeking to understand. Indeed, we might go as far as to say that data generation and analyses are reliant upon our abilities to craft meaningful relations and on our understanding of how those relations are locally and culturally framed.

Of course, as in life, not all relationships of fieldwork are positive, life affirming or necessarily productive. I have already indicated that relations can become strained or complicated; moreover, fieldwork relations often occupy a plane between reality and falsehood. They are false in that they are often, at least initially, contrived by the researcher in order to accomplish the research. However, contrived does not necessarily imply a lack of mutual respect or genuine feeling. Ethnographers can be genuine in wanting to develop mutually meaningful relationships. Equally, informants can develop mutual respect and come to share understandings of the value of good relationships for 'telling their story' or sharing their social world. However, there are constraints in field relationships. All parties might see benefit in maintaining relationships as 'work', as part of a research project where researcher and participants all have a stake. However, we cannot and should not conceive of such relationships simply as purposive work. Relations borne out of ethnographic fieldwork can and do have real emotional purchase; the consequences and impacts of our fieldwork relationships are significant. Ethnographers have written about genuine friendships, commitment and even love they have found during fieldwork; and where that has diminished there have equally been real feelings of anguish, guilt, betrayal and hurt, even hate (see Coffey, 1999).

Ethnographers rarely accomplish fieldwork without being affected in some way by the experience. The nature of fieldwork, with its inherently relational qualities, almost always requires some level of emotional investment. It is important, therefore, that we recognize the necessity to view the relations of fieldwork as both personal and professional – guided by different rules than our purely personal relationships, but relations that are not crafted impersonally. The relational aspects of fieldwork involve pragmatic as well as emotional production.

LEAVING THE FIELD

Relatively little attention has been paid in the methods literature to leaving the field or ending fieldwork, compared, for example, with what has been written on access and entry to the field. Where researchers have paid particular attention to documenting the end of fieldwork, it is usually where the research has been particularly emotional and where leaving has been especially difficult. For example, Cannon (1992) wrote a particularly moving account of ending her fieldwork with women who had cancer, and where she had built up personal friendships which she did not want to leave behind. When Cannon ended her research she felt that she could not completely leave the field; the friendships forged and emotional investment for Cannon and her informants were significant and transcended the context of the specific research encounter.

Where advice is offered on leaving the field, this errs towards the pragmatic rather than the personal. Of course, there are useful markers of etiquette associated with ending a research project, because time has run out or due to other similar research imperatives. For example, Lofland and Lofland (1995) offered a range of practical advice in relation to saying goodbye to a research setting and participants. This advice included making people aware of your plans in good time, avoiding leaving too abruptly and/or without explanation, explaining what you are doing next, saying goodbye in person where possible, and promising to keep in touch (and then doing so where appropriate and possible). This all seems like sound advice. Leaving the field should be planned for carefully, wherever possible, in just the same way that access is usually managed with care. Ending fieldwork should always be done with courtesy. However, it is also important to recognize that leaving the field can be an emotional experience, even where field-work has not seemed to be particularly emotional. It can, of course, be something of a relief to finish fieldwork, and it is OK to feel relieved. Fieldwork is arduous work, time consuming, tiring, and intellectually and physically draining. We can also experience a range of other emotions as fieldwork comes to an end. Leaving the field can mean leaving people, sometimes friends, and also often marks an epiphany in our own career or life. Doctoral students in social anthropology, for example, have described a post fieldwork phase imbued with a sense of strange-ness and personal loss (Coffey and Atkinson, 1996). Returning from the field can signify the end of an era and the beginning of a new phase of your work, career and life. For some, where fieldwork has taken them away from home, leaving the field can also involve a physical act of moving, packing up possessions and mov-ing home or moving back. For all of us, the end of fieldwork means moving on. Stebbins (1991) has argued that we never really leave the field, and that we always remain somehow connected and involved. Fieldwork becomes, and is part of, who we are and will always be. The very act of leaving, though, enables us to remember and to reflect – on the place, the people, the time and our sense of self. Leaving can also mean getting to know the field in a new way, through reading, revisit-ing and analyzing our field notes and transcripts, as well as through our writing practices. In that sense, the ending of fieldwork may not really signify 'leaving the field'. But it does provide physical and temporal separation, and the demarcation of a new kind of relationship with a setting and with social actors in that setting, perhaps based on remembering, retelling and representing.

Despite best advice, leaving the field can be protracted and messy, perhaps with no clear moment of disassociation. For some there can be a drifting apart rather than a clear-cut act of leaving. Most endings, though, are phased and on a continuum rather than fieldwork planned to come to an abrupt end. But even in the cases where the end of fieldwork is phased, it is important to prepare for leaving the field and for thinking about the management of relationships and selves post-fieldwork. There is a physicality to fieldwork, the very act of being there provides embodied structure and meaning; ending fieldwork requires a reorientation. In some ways we never leave the field, as that would mean leaving our pasts and our memories, and something of ourselves behind. The significant of leaving is interwoven with what that symbolizes. Leaving means we were there.

A NOTE ON ETHNOGRAPHY AND AUTOBIOGRAPHY

In this chapter I have focused on the roles and relations of ethnographic fieldwork, and have argued that we should not separate ourselves from the settings and people we study. There are important affordances in recognizing that the researcher is central to ethnographic work, and in working productively at understanding the mutual relationships between researcher and the places and people in which and with whom fieldwork takes place. This, then, makes a case for understanding and reflecting on the self as part of the research process.

There are contemporary ethnographic practices which have recast the self even more firmly in the context of ethnography. **Autoethnography** (sometimes referred to as ethno-autobiography) refers to a distinctive form of research practice that focuses on ethnography as autobiography; that is, using ethnographic method and sensibilities to explicitly and self-consciously research the self (Ellis and Bochner, 2006). This refers not so much to the act of ethnographic research itself, but rather to the writing of ethnographic texts as a means to understanding our own life experiences. Autoethnography takes our own experiences and subjects them to ethnographic analysis (see Chapter 8, this volume). However, it worth contending here, that all ethnographic work involves some level of *autobiographical* practice, whether or not we subscribe to *autoethnographic* practice. The lives of ethnographers are lived through, and in relation to, the fieldwork they undertake; data collection, analysis and writing draw on and are influenced by the lives that have been lived and are being lived by ethnographers undertaking those tasks. This is distinctive from research and writing projects that start from the self and our own experiences. Drawing on our own experiences and lives can be productive, in terms of providing us with a lens through which to experience and make sense of complex social worlds. Starting from where we are can also be productive in terms of selecting research topics and settings that have personal meanings or investments for us. The key here though remains being reflexive of the relationships between our lives and those other lives we seek to understand, together with an ethnographic imperative to make sense of complex social worlds through a combination of experience and observation.

● KEY POINTS

- Ethnography relies on the researcher being able to establish roles and relationships within a setting.
- The ethnographer brings their personal characteristics, experiences and markers of identity to the research. These need to be acknowledged and reflected upon in context of fieldwork. Our identities can limit or enhance the possibilities of fieldwork.
- The roles that can be adopted in ethnography can be multiple and varied. They will include more or less participation in the everyday social world of the setting, and may vary over time or in relation to different groups or regions of a setting.
- Ethnographic fieldwork is relational and personal. The relationships that are forged in the field can impact upon our experiences, understandings and sense of self. Ethnographic friendships can be complex.
- Leaving the field is an important part of the ethnographic process.
- Ethnographic research can be considered as a form of autobiographical practice, in which and through which lives are lived.

■ FURTHER READING

Coffey, A. (1999) *The Ethnographic Self: Fieldwork and the Representation of Identity.* London: Sage.

Davies, C.A. (2008) *Reflexive Ethnography: A Guide to Researching Selves and Others*, 2nd ed. Abingdon, Oxon and New York: Routledge.

Ellis, C. (2004) *The Ethnographic I: A Methodological Novel about Autoethnography.* Walnut Creek, CA: AltaMira Press.

CHAPTER SIX

MANAGING AND ANALYZING ETHNOGRAPHIC DATA

CONTENTS

OBJECTIVES

After reading this chapter, you will:

- have a better understanding of the relationships between data collection, data analysis and the development of theory in ethnography;
- have an awareness of the ways in which data management can support the analytical task;
- be able to identify complementary strategies for ethnographic data analysis;
- be able to describe how patterns and themes can be identified and interrogated through data analysis;
- have an appreciation of the different ways in which narrative and spoken data are analyzed; and
- be able to identify opportunities afforded by computer-aided analysis of qualitative data.

BEGINNING DATA ANALYSIS

Data analysis (see also Gibbs, 2018) is not, and should not be, a distinctive phase in ethnographic research. Rather there is an ongoing dialogue between data collection and data analysis; a process which allows the researcher to work back and forth – from gathering data, to organizing data into an order that supports the generation of ideas, and onwards to further data collection to explore and develop those ideas and so on. Indeed analysis of sorts actually begins prior to data collection in ethnography, as we scope out and undertake preliminary investigation in order to plan fieldwork. We usually begin to have ideas about, and in relation to, the field before we go about the task of systematically gathering data. In ethnographic research there is an imperative to begin by considering a wide frame, and then progressively focus our data collection in the field, as we develop ideas and gain analytical purchase. Over time, and as our understanding of the research setting grows, we will focus our activities, become more purposive in our data gathering and fine tune the scope of our investigations. This process of progressive focus relies on an early intellectual engagement with our data, and on the adoption of strategies that facilitate the development of ideas. This work, for it is work to be worked on, is analysis. In practice, it can be difficult to develop a systematic and orderly approach to data analysis while fieldwork is ongoing. Fieldwork can be intense and time consuming; often our research design does not or cannot build in sufficient periods for sustained analytical reflection during data collection. Indeed it can be very difficult to process and organize all of our data (which might incorporate combinations of notes, transcripts, documents, visual materials, audio recordings and other material traces) on an ongoing basis during fieldwork. However, it is important that fieldwork always encompasses some level of reflexivity and thinking time; that the generation of ideas emergent from data gathered begins early and takes place often; and hence that the analytical work is not parked until we have left the field. It is difficult to test ideas, pursue new lines of inquiry and follow up interesting points in our data once we are no longer in a position to engage with the setting through fieldwork, and the opportunities that presents for further data collection. All of that said, the systematic and final analysis of ethnographic data will follow on from intense periods of fieldwork data collection. Systematic attention to data, using a variety of strategies to categorize, display and retrieve material collected in the field, provides the framework and space to think about and to think with our data. Data analysis entails seeking out productive ways of organizing and reorganizing data in order to generate themes and concepts, which might have explanatory as well as descriptive value.

There are a number of ways of undertaking data analysis in ethnography, and a variety of approaches can be utilized to aid the analytical task. The choice of analytical strategy is a personal one, but should always be principled and based on an understanding of the alternative strategies that are available or possible. Moreover, there needs to be an awareness that the choices in analysis will also have an impact on the outcomes of our research, framing what it is possible to say about the setting under study. Analysis is a process through which data are interpreted and theories are derived and tested. Interpretation will lead to different levels of description – enabling the identification of patterns, themes, and indeed irregularities, and the construction of rich descriptive accounts. A significant amount of ethnographic work stops at the level of description; there is much of value in being able to offer empirically informed thick description of settings and social actors, as a way of providing analytical insight into everyday worlds. However, it is also possible to go beyond description with ethnographic analysis, developing theoretical or explanatory concepts that begin to account for, as well as to describe, the phenomenon under study.

As has been noted, ethnographic data can take a number of forms; there is variety in the materials that are generated and collected through ethnographic research practice. Any one dataset might include field notes, interview transcripts, photographs, film, sound recordings, artefacts and documents. There is also variety in the approaches, practices and methods that can be employed to analyze those data. Analytical approaches provide vehicles to combine art and science, both important to ethnographic work. Ethnographic analysis is artful in that it is creative and can be playful. Analysis uses our imagination. Though potentially creative, imaginative and expansive, analysis is achieved through systematic, robust techniques and practices.

Metaphorically speaking, in analysis, it is important to show our 'workings' – that is, to be clear how we have worked with our data in order to reach our interpretations and conclusions. Creative, systematic analysis is capable of developing both description and interpretation of data in ways that capture the complexities and nuances of our research settings. In describing the analysis of qualitative data more generally, Tesch (1990), identified a number of common features that transcend any particular analytical technique that is chosen. Analysis should be cyclical and reflexive; systematic but not rigid. Analysis provides opportunities for data to be divided into meaningful units, but in ways that maintain some connection to the whole. Analysis is data led, organized in such a way as to derive from data themselves. Data analysis in qualitative research should be methodical but flexible, imaginative as well as rigorous.

In this chapter, what follows is a description of some of the techniques of, and approaches to, the analysis of ethnographic data, drawing on principles and practices of qualitative inquiry. The intention is to show that there are principled choices that can be made in relation to data analysis in ethnography, and that different approaches will lend themselves to different kinds of analytical work and interpretation. The focus of the chapter here is primarily on the analysis of textual ethnographic data (for example, field notes, transcripts and documents), rather than on other modes of data (for example, visual data). However, the overarching principles introduced are applicable across the full range of data types. The chapter also considers the relationship between analyzing and theorizing, as well as addressing how ethnographic data analysis can be aided by computer software (see also Gibbs, 2018).

A NOTE ON DATA ORGANIZATION AND MANAGEMENT

Over the course of an ethnographic research project it is important that data are organized and managed in ways that will facilitate analysis and the generation of ideas. Data may include field notes, interview transcriptions, documents collected in the field, as well as perhaps photographs and other artefacts of fieldwork. An ethnographic dataset can also include analytical notes we might make during the course of our research. As we go about the business of writing up field notes, or reading documents of or about the field of study, or listening to and transcribing ethnographic interviews, we will already start to have analytical ideas. It is useful that we note and record these ideas as we go along. Such analytic notes can be used to inform further data collection, and will also prove to be helpful adjuncts to data during the main phase of analysis.

In relation to ethnographic data management, a good starting point is to put in place a scheme to organize data chronologically. This is a good habit to get into from the start of a research project. However, as a project progresses, it might be useful to think of organizing data in other ways; perhaps broadly by theme, or different regions of a setting, or social groups within that setting, or some other set of categories that seems a sensible way of organizing what might be a complex and multi-faceted set of data. It is important that such categorization is helpful in organizing data meaningfully (data management must make sense to the ethnographer), and in ways that will aid data retrieval and systematic analysis, both during fieldwork and afterwards. It is worth noting that these initial and ongoing organization strategies are actually part of the analytical process. In order to organize and manage data, it is necessary to engage in a dialogue with those data, seeking out ways to present and re-present data that are based on our ideas of what might be useful ways of categorizing and describing the field.

Many ethnographers now utilize computers and digital technology to store and manage data, which might be multimodal in form. Many general and readily accessible computer software packages (for example, routine word processing and spreadsheet applications) have good capability, and come with functions that assist with the storage, organization and manipulation of textual and visual data. There are also a range of bespoke software applications that are designed specifically to support the management and analysis of qualitative data. Regardless of their analytical potential (of which more later in this chapter), such applications provide a variety of frameworks and structures for managing and organizing complex qualitative datasets in ways that support the close reading and re-reading of data. But it is not essential to utilize computer technologies to manage ethnographic data. It is entirely possible, of course, to organize data files manually. This might include recourse to index cards, paper files or folders, colour coding or other forms of tagging. There might also be occasions in the field where it might not be possible or desirable to use computers and/or to generate data in digital form; though there is a distinction to be made between data that we generate in the field, and the data that we reconstruct and elaborate upon outside of the fieldwork. Field notes, for example, might include notebooks full of pencil jottings, scribbles and sketches, as well as richly descriptive processed notes, which have been worked up, worked on and typed following fieldwork. Our systems for organizing data need to take into account the different forms and modes of data, and the possibilities for working across and between data that are presented in different ways. Whatever the different kinds of ethnographic data that are presented, or personal preferences for data management, the principles remain the same. Data are best organized and stored in systematic and methodical ways, but not so rigidly as to close down new areas for data display and representation during the analytical task. Data management in ethnography should:

- Be planned in advance.
- Be undertaken during fieldwork, not left to the end of fieldwork.
- Be systematic and flexible.
- Enable easy retrieval and manipulation of data.
- Facilitate varieties of data display.

LOOKING FOR PATTERNS AND MEANING

Analysis of ethnographic data often begins with the identification of themes and patterns. This usually entails developing a practical strategy for coding and categorizing the data, based on the identification of potentially meaningful concepts or ideas. Thematic analysis of this kind relies on segmenting what is often a large and complex dataset into smaller and more manageable units for analysis. This process is often termed 'code-and-retrieve', indicating that it involves using 'codes' (for example, categories, indices, themes) in order to label and organize data in some way, and then being able to 'retrieve' (find or group) data according to those assigned codes. The term 'coding' can imply a process that is rather rudimentary and mechanistic. Coding (see also Flick, 2018d; Gibbs, 2018) can actually be rather complex, creative and detailed. It is important, however, to note that coding is not in and of itself data analysis; rather coding provides a means of subjecting data to close and critical scrutiny, and serves as a precursory process through which concepts and ideas can be generated.

Assigning codes or labels to data provides the opportunity to think about data in constituent parts, but also enables us to develop links across and between data. Charmaz describes coding as 'naming segments of data with a label that simultaneously categorizes, summarizes, and accounts for each piece of data' (2006, p. 43). Data segments can then be brought together and linked in new ways as a result of coding. Such linkage does not necessarily need to be chronological or sequential. Linkages can be made between different data units in order to develop concepts, explore hierarchies, look for patterns and consider irregularities or exceptions. It is these data linkages between codes and categories that underpin the analytical work associated with coding; that is how codes and categories are actively worked in order to interrogate and interpret the data to hand.

There are a variety of approaches that can be used to undertake, and indeed conceptualize, coding in ethnographic and qualitative research. Miles and Huberman described coding as the very 'stuff of analysis' (1994, p. 56), and stressed the value of coding in enabling data to be differentiated and combined in ways that aided critical reflection. Coding in this formulation is a process to enable meaningful data to be identified and organized prior to interpretation. From this perspective, coding can provide a way of simplifying data; acting as a form of indexation in order to reduce data to key points and concepts. One result of this approach is that qualitative data can be treated quasi-quantitatively. For example, it is possible and can be useful to count instances of phenomena and map the relative occurrence of different codes across a dataset. Seidel and Kelle (1995) note that, from such a perspective, codes are used heuristically, as we are not just 'counting' in any overly simple numerical or abstract sense. Rather, the 'reduction' of data to codes and categories, and then using this simplification to identify patterns of practice, provides opportunities to explore, investigate, challenge and re-code data.

Of course, coding does not just simplify or reduce data to constituent parts. Coding also enables researchers to 'scrutinize and interact with the data, as well as ask analytical questions of the data' (Thornberg and Charmaz, 2014, p. 156). Coding can be used to reconceptualize, open up, transform and rethink data. Strauss (1987), for example, was very clear that coding is an analytical procedure through which data can be complicated and expanded. Strauss considered 'coding' to be a significant part of the analytic task in qualitative research. He linked an initial coding process (which he referred to as open coding), to a more detailed and nuanced process of using coding to generate conceptual frameworks (Strauss and Corbin 1990; see also Glaser, 2001). From this perspective, coding leads to questioning and speculation and on to what Strauss referred to as axial coding – where coding and the manipulation of codes enable the exploration of factors such as the consequences and antecedents of data and of fieldwork itself. From this viewpoint, coding is more than simply assigning categories to data, and is certainly more than 'counting' relevant phenomena. Sensitive and detailed coding can lead to conceptualization, questioning and discovery, through a close reading of and attention to the nuances of data.

The codes and categories that we might apply to our data can come from a number of sources. There are no hard and fast rules in relation to what are appropriate coding frameworks and what are not, though a good degree of reflection is always important. Most especially so that we don't start to overlook or ignore aspects of our data that don't seem to 'fit' with our coding strategy, but also so we don't take a line of least resistance – adopting codes just because they seem self-evident or obvious. A coding framework might initially be developed based on a first and cursory reading of the data, and in relation to what immediately presents as potentially interesting to the researcher. Particular events, activities, words, people, places or processes might appear in, or indeed leap from, the data themselves, and this is often as good a place as any to start. There are, however, plenty of other ways in which a coding frame might be developed, and in practice we might use a variety of strategies for generating codes over the course of analysis. For example, categories and coding frames can come from:

- Foreshadowed research questions or problems identified prior to fieldwork.
- Previous research or studies in the field, or research that is in some way comparable.
- Concepts derived from the research literature.
- Existing theoretical or conceptual frameworks.
- Local categories used by social actors themselves or otherwise present in the field.

These are merely suggestions. It is important to note that there are no right or wrong ways of developing or applying codes. Coding and categorizing data are tools to think with and should be selected by the researcher for that purpose. Codes and categories are created by the researcher and can be modified, changed, expanded, or indeed abandoned, as we work at and with our data. Coding is an aid to analysis and interpretation; a means to an end rather than an end in itself. Codes can be applied, interrogated, questioned and revised. Coding also and often goes hand-in-hand with strategies for data display. Thinking of ways in which data might be displayed, including in relation to the codes and categories we are using and the themes that are emerging through that coding process, can be a useful way of paying close attention to data and to the relationships within and across our dataset. There are a range of possibilities for data display for ethnographic and qualitative data. For example, matrices and tables can be very useful ways to display coding frameworks, allowing shorthand ways of exploring comparisons of simple relationships. Similarly, tree-structures and other more complex diagrams can be used to display potentially different levels of data, presenting opportunities to explore hierarchical or other relationships with our coding frameworks.

Code-and-retrieve processes are valuable ways of managing and organizing ethnographic data, and for exploring relationships within and across data. Data coding has been particularly well served by the development of computer-aided strategies for qualitative data analysis. Bespoke software has been developed and used for more than the last 30 years, and contemporary applications support increasingly sophisticated ways of data organization, management and display (Silver and Lewins, 2014; see also later in this chapter). However, while coding and categorizing data to support data management and thematic analysis are prominent within ethnographic research, there are other strategies for analysis that can also be utilized.

NARRATIVES, METAPHORS AND SYMBOLS

The analytical task in ethnography can be supported by a range of strategies and techniques, which particularly focus on interview, conversational or documentary data. Narrative analysis is one such approach to the treatment of qualitative data, which lends itself well to the analysis of accounts of experience. Hence the strategies for the analysis of narratives provide possible approaches to the interrogation of ethnographic interviews and conversations. As ethnographers, we will often collect narratives and stories from our informants. This might occur 'naturally' during 'everyday' conversations that are often an integral part of fieldwork, or accounts might be more purposively generated through planned research interviews. The storied or narrative qualities of conversational and ethnographic interview data present opportunities for analysis – drawing on formal linguistic narrative analysis, as well as on other ways of understanding narrative form and function. Such analysis does not rely on a fine segmentation or coding of data; rather there is an emphasis on treating larger units of data (such as a whole interview, or a substantial part of an interview) as a distinct entity. In so doing, narrative analysis can assist with the development of understanding how accounts are constructed, as well as in the roles accounts might play in describing and making sense of experience.

There are formal approaches to the literary analysis of narratives and stories, drawing on the work of sociolinguistics. The approach developed by Labov is one such example, and has been used within qualitative research (Labov, 1972, 1982; see Cortazzi, 1993, for a practice example). Labov paid particular attention to the linguistic characteristics of narratives, developing a framework for considering their formal structures and properties, as well as the social functions that narratives might serve. Sociolinguistics recognizes that narrative structures have repeating and recognizable patterns, and that paying attention to these patterns can provide a means of interpreting narrative forms. While qualitative researchers, have developed a range of approaches to narrative analysis (see Elliott, 2005; Riessman, 1993), that go beyond simply an attention to structure, there is a general agreement by researchers interested in accounts that attending to the structure of a narrative account can be helpful – not least because it forces a broader analytical focus on what is said, how it is being said, and indeed why it is being said. Questions which ask what, how and why all might be of interest to the ethnographer researcher intent on making sense of social settings from the perspectives of social actors in the field.

The model developed by Labov provides a framework for unpacking and interrogating narrative structure and function. It does so through posing a series of questions; these questions enable a focus on the units of a narrative structure, and, importantly, on how these units work together in useful and meaningful ways in order to 'do' and 'make sense' of social and cultural life. In terms of structure, Labov (1972) indicated that narratives will often begin with an 'abstract' – a statement which provides some opening contextualization, signalling the start of a story, and perhaps indicating what and who the narrative is going to be about. Most narratives will then seek to 'orientate' the audience – providing information that enables the account to be situated within its social context. To interrogate an account we can look for signs of this orientation – asking questions such as 'Who is this account about?'; 'What is the account about?'; 'When did what is being described take place?'; 'Where did it happen?'.

Following orientation, Labov's model looks for the 'complication'; this is the core of the account, and where we get to ask questions like 'What happened?'; 'What transpired?'; 'What took place and how did it come about?'. In looking for and identifying answers to these questions we can start to explore not only how but why the account is being told. In Labov's model, after complication comes 'evaluation' – this is where we look for aspects of the narrative where purpose is stated, though this might be in subtle and nuanced ways. In interrogating the narrative in terms of its evaluative purpose, we might pose such questions as 'So what?'; 'Why does it matter?'; 'Why are you telling (me) this?'. Narratives also have endings – and we can pay analytical attention to these. Following Labov's framework, endings will includes the 'result' ('So what was the outcome?'; 'How did it end?'; 'Where did things finish up?'), and may also include a 'coda' (a turn of phrase or sentence, or non-verbal sign, which signals that the narrative has ended).

Our analytical concern here is not with a hard and fast linear or chronological ordering of these narrative units; indeed over the course of a 'story' recounted in an interview or conversation, each of these narrative elements might occur and recur several times. Stories might include a number of 'complications' and 'evaluations', before getting to any 'results'. Stories can be layered and multifaceted. There can be stories within stories. Rather, the analytical affordance of paying attention to narrative structure is that it provides a way of subjecting our data to careful and systematic scrutiny, providing a framework for thinking about and working with our data. In that sense, narrative analysis is not so very different from ethnographic thematic analysis using codes and categories. Labov's framework for narrative analysis, even very simply applied, enables us to reflect on how accounts, perhaps generated through ethnographic interviews or conversations, are structured, and also offers a mechanism through which we might then reflect upon the reasons for, or functions of, the story. This returns to our analytical imperative in ethnography – in thinking about the structure and function of 'telling', we are able to gain insights into the everyday accounting practices and socially constituted realities of our informants and participants.

Narratives are situated within particular social and cultural contexts, and are told with implicit or explicit purpose. Thus, it can be analytically useful and significant to further explore the functional qualities of accounts generated and collected during fieldwork. Narratives can provide a way of chronicling life experience through a shared frame of reference. Narratives can validate, celebrate, warn or shame. They can be boastful or self-referential. They can share success, help to explain failure and be recounted as a kind of morality tale. The point here is that we should not be seeking to impose meaning through a kind of overly simplistic analysis or based on our own assumptions. Rather, we should be alert to the analytical affordance of paying close and systematic attention to 'the ways of' and 'reasons for telling' as part of ethnographic research practice, especially where our methods have generated data in narrative form.

A focus on narrative indicates analytical interest in the use of language by social actors in the field. How social actors convey meaning through language can be explored in a variety of ways. For example, spoken interaction draws on and is constructed through linguistic, rhetorical and semantic devices, and focusing on these can yield insightful analysis. Perhaps particularly so when analyzing ethnographic data derived from 'naturally occurring' interaction in the field, though such attention to linguistic detail can also be relevant in the analysis of ethnographic interview data and even documents from the field. Metaphorical devices, such as tropes, similes, analogies and other figurative imagery, are a good case in point. Metaphors can be described as linguistic devices of representation. Using metaphors enables social actors to draw on shared characteristics and understandings. In analytical terms metaphors can be explored from various positions. For example, we can explore the perceived intention of the metaphor, the semantic mode that is being used and the cultural context of the metaphorical statement. We might find analytical interest in the function of the metaphoric device (what is it being used to 'do'?), as well as the meaning or meanings inherent in its usage. The use of metaphor in social interactions, and in research encounters, can be revealing, particular so if we think of the cultural and social contexts within which metaphors are used. Metaphors can provide ways of expressing shared knowledge, values and identities; thus metaphors can be interrogated in terms of the language/terminology used and the shared characteristics or knowledges that are implied, as well as the ways in which metaphors are structured, deployed and performed in everyday practice.

Metaphors are one way of exploring language and vocabulary as a means of developing analytical understanding of the field under study. Language more generally is used in particular ways to convey shared meanings, and hence can be of significant interest to ethnographers. Metaphors are but one example of the wide-ranging use of linguistic 'symbols' in social and cultural contexts. We can therefore develop and extend our ethnographic attention to language through a fuller, more fine-grained exploration of the signs and symbols imbued through and in language in everyday social life. For instance, in some settings and circumstances there might be analytical value in focusing on the 'folk terms' used by social actors: specific language and terms that are particular to that setting; the linguistic symbols that are used, their terms of reference, when they are brought to bear; and how local meanings become encoded in and through such linguistic devices. Referred to more formally as 'domain analysis', this detailed approach to local and situated language provides a particular way of exploring the tacit cultural knowledge of the field setting. In so doing there is a focus on language as an enactment of culture. There are formal and technical ways in which domain analysis can be undertaken, enabling taxonomies and network relations to be mapped (see Spradley, 1979; Coffey and Atkinson, 1996). Such techniques expand on the general principle of recognizing local terms and vernacular language as a means to exploring and understanding everyday social contexts and enactments. There is significant analytical affordance in ethnography to be had in exploring the research setting through its own linguistic terms, though we should always be mindful of not imposing our own meanings and imagery. The strength of an ethnographic focus on language is in exploring how social actors themselves attach meanings to their language and forms of expression. Such an approach can be utilized reflexively to situate local language within its social and cultural context.

ANALYZING AND THEORIZING

Theorizing is a key aspect of data analysis in ethnographic work. Indeed we should not conceive of theorizing as a separate activity, distinct from data analysis (or indeed as an activity which is isolated from research design and data collection). In ethnography, strategies and techniques for data analysis provide us with opportunities to 'think about' and to 'think with' our data. This thinking process can be based on systematic, analytical engagement with data, but should also be creative and artful, enabling ideas to be generated and played with. Ideas are the foundation stones and building blocks of theory. A close attention to our data, through processes and techniques of analysis, enable us to think with and about our data. Theorizing also means to extend and go beyond our data, developing, using and testing ideas that enable further engagement with the field of study. In this context, the definition of theory provided by Dey (1993) is a helpful one. Dey described theory 'simply as an idea about how other ideas might be related'. Taking this as a starting point, we can readily see how the processes of analyzing and theorizing are interwoven in ethnographic practice. Of course, ideas are integral to the whole ethnographic enterprise. We use our own ideas, along with those of other scholars, to develop our foreshadowed questions, to select our research site or topic of interest, and to inform our data collection strategy in the field. Our ideas (our theories) will also inform our analytical strategy and the ways in which we go about identifying and codifying insights – we will develop our own ideas of what is going on in the field and will want to test those ideas alongside those of our key informants and other participants in the field. We also know that we bring to our research established and emergent theoretical frameworks. Such frameworks can be used to inform, challenge and conceptualize data collection, data analysis and our research experience. Such theoretical frameworks can include schools of thought through which ethnography is often and most readily situated – for example, interactionism, phenomenology, feminism and critical studies (see Chapter 1, this volume), but also other, diverse approaches (for example, psychosocial studies – see Woodward, 2015). Using ideas – theories – implicitly as well as explicitly, is an integral part of the ethnographic research process. We build ideas into data collection and data analysis; we expand and test existing ideas as well as generating new ideas to describe and attempt to explain what is happening in the social worlds we are seeking to understand. Theorizing is an especially important part of our processes of interpretation and analysis. More formally, it is helpful to consider the ways in which theory in relation to ethnographic work can take on a number of guises, and also enable us to contribute to theory in a variety of ways.

It is helpful to distinguish between substantive and formal theory in the context of ethnographic work (Glaser and Strauss, 1967). In ethnography, theorizing most often begins at the substantive level, and in so doing is concerned with attempting to make sense of very particular local contexts. In order to do this we interrogate data borne of specific settings in order to generate ideas about what is happening 'here and now'. Indeed a quality of ethnographic research is its capacity to develop nuanced and richly evidenced ideas – theoretical understandings if you will – of the local and the particular. However, it is important not to lose sight of the opportunities that ethnographic research provides to generate (or contribute to) more generalized or formal theory. That is, theorization that has analytical purchase and capacity beyond the specific localized context (Urquhart, 2012). While specific ethnographic data are there to think with and to think about, our analyses and ideas will make contributions beyond those data. Indeed ethnographic data collection and data analysis are perhaps best seen in relation to, rather than separate from, disciplinary and theoretical frameworks. An overly narrow view of data analysis does not do duty to the broader goals of ethnographic research – to develop understanding, discovery and interpretation of complex social worlds. Ethnographic research is practised in specific fields or research settings, but can speak to wider concerns and understandings.

In ethnography, moving from a preoccupation with the management and inter-rogation of data towards interpretation and theorization is an important step. The ways in which we generate, develop, harness and use ideas is a key ethnographic imperative, and of course is something we all routinely do in our own everyday lives. However, making the processes of generating and testing ideas explicit is often diffi-cult to do, though vital in the research process. Peirce's notion of abductive reasoning is helpful here (Peirce, 1979; see also Kelle, 1995). Abductive reasoning can be used heuristically and in analytically productive ways as part of ethnographic research practice. Abductive logic is also at the heart of 'grounded theorizing', though it is not necessary to endorse a grounded theory approach in ethnography (see Charmaz and Mitchell (2001) for a discussion of the relationship between grounded theory and ethnography). Peirce uses abductive reasoning as a means by which to contrast inductive and deductive logic. Inductive approaches to theorization presume that generalizations are developed through the gathering of cases, with patterns (as well as irregularities) revealed through more and more data observations until a point of saturation. This, though, can rather unhelpfully lead to a mentality of ever more cases to be collected – ever more observations, conversations and interviews to be undertaken and analyzed, and a fearfulness of stopping for fear of missing data that just might be significant. In such cases, inductive reasoning can lead to analysis that struggles to go beyond description. On the other hand, recourse to deductive logic can be just as stifling, with data collection limited by and to the testing of existing theories, without the opportunities for creativity and innovative theoreti-cal development. Neither inductive nor deductive reasoning provides a particularly good basis for ethnographic research. Both limit the artful and creative exploration of theory development. Abductive reasoning provides a possible alternative theoretical approach from which to work. Abductive reasoning starts unapologetically with the local and the particular (for example, a specific setting or field of study), and therefore sits well with ethnography. Through close attention to data, phenomena of interest are identified. This might be something that is surprising or unusual or intriguing, or perhaps something that seems to be happening a lot or at particular times. These phenomena are then interrogated and explored, but always in relation to broader concepts and bodies of knowledge. This might include existing theoretical frame-works, disciplinary models, comparable data or experiences from elsewhere, other fieldwork, or our own experiences and positionalities. Hence, there is explicit and purposeful intent from the start that we are interrogating and working with our data in relation to wider theoretical, conceptual and interpretive frameworks. There is an open dialogic process at work that serves to stretch our thinking beyond the specific and the particular. This does not mean simply slotting our data and our thinking into existing frameworks of analysis and interpretation, nor using data explicitly to debunk or catch out existing theories. Rather, abductive reasoning recognizes the productive interplay of and between existing ideas and findings, new data and new ideas. This presents and represents an open, exploratory spirit within which ethnographic work can productively operate. In ethnography, theories can be used heuristically; theorization extends rather than limits our thinking; using ideas is a creative process.

COMPUTER-AIDED ANALYSIS

The analysis of qualitative data, including theorization and theory building, can be supported by a range of computational software. Indeed many aspects of data management and data analysis outlined in this chapter can be underpinned by careful and appropriate use of technology (see also Gibbs, 2018). It is important to note, however, that while generic and bespoke software packages can complement and support processes of qualitative analysis, computer software cannot do the thinking work that is required. Even the most sophisticated qualitative data analysis software cannot 'choose' which analytical strategy or technique might work best in relation to your particular dataset or foreshadowed problems. Nor can any software package actually do the analysis work for us. The intellectual work of analysis cannot be undertaken by software. Analytical choices are still ours to identify and to make. What computer software does provide is a range of options for helping us to organize and manage our data, and for applying systematic approaches to the practical tasks of analysis (Silver and Lewins, 2014). This can be particularly helpful when ethnographic projects generate significant amounts of data, and/or data in a number of different forms. Of course digital and computational methods have also had a transformative impact on ethnographic research (and indeed social research more generally), including providing new online settings for data collection, enabling the generation of new forms of data collection (for example, through social media), and routinizing the capturing and storing of data electronically as text and media files (for more on ethnography in the digital age see Boellstorff et al., 2012; Dicks et al., 2005; Hallett and Barber, 2014; Hine, 2000).

There is a wide range of generally available computer software that can be of value in managing and analyzing ethnographic data. Standard word processing packages, for example, enable textual data to be prepared, stored and retrieved with ease. Spreadsheet packages can facilitate simple coding frames and be used to capture metadata. And there are a variety of readily available visualization and graphics packages available that can assist with data display. It is now also possible to use mainstream and routinely used software to store, manipulate and retrieve visual and sound data with relative ease. The omnipresence of mobile devices, and our increased abilities to operate digitally in our everyday lives, have also made the task of data recording, retrieval and display, including for ethnographic research purposes, easier and more accessible, without the necessity of bespoke packages or complex training. Indeed many of us are increasingly self-taught users of complex technologies in our everyday lives. Computational capacity and digital platforms can also facilitate research management; for example, enabling remote working (which might be particularly relevant for ethnographers in the field), collaboration, team working and the sharing of data and ongoing analyses.

Beyond an increasingly normalized and routine use of general computer and digital software, the last 30 years have seen a burgeoning of dedicated software packages to support analysis and theory building specifically for qualitative research. Computer-aided qualitative data analysis has been and is supported by a whole suite of software packages specifically designed to store, manage and manipulate qualitative data, including data that comes in different modes and forms. Most of these packages work on variations of a model of thematic analysis, drawing on code-and–retrieve sensibilities. Some packages enable non-textual data to be tagged, facilitate the inclusion of visual and sound data in data display and provide structures to help the development of connections and linkages between data in order to develop hierarchical or other relationships as an aid to theory building. Many follow a grounded theory approach to qualitative research. Over time, these bespoke packages have become increasingly sophisticated, and new editions seem to always be in development. Contemporary versions of software packages to support qualitative data analysis include *The Ethnograph*, *Atlas.ti* and *NVivo*, all of which have lineages stretching back to the start of qualitative analysis software (Silver and Lewins, 2014).

There has been a move in recent years to encourage qualitative data analysis via a bespoke software package, and almost a glorification of computer-aided qualitative data analysis software (**CAQDAS**). It is, of course, important and sensible that there is an awareness of how computer software can support data management, analysis and theory building in ethnography. However, it is equally important that we guard against the development of some kind of mono-orthodoxy based on the procedures and assumptions that are inherent in many, if not most, contemporary dedicated software applications (for example, code-and-retrieve and grounded theory as standard). Computational strategies and software can aid and complement our analytical approaches, but they are not and cannot be substitutes for the process of analysis and the generation of ideas. Software of various kinds can play an important part in assisting with data storage, management and efficient data retrieval, as well as providing interesting and creative opportunities for data display. But the analytical capacity of all or any software is still dependent on the researcher generating the ideas for analysis and creating the codes, categories or other ways of interrogating the data. At the very least, ethnographic researchers should appreciate and understand what packages are available, and how they might assist with the processes of data management, data display and systematic data analysis. Ethnographers though should remain mindful of the debates about qualitative data analysis software. While there have been concerns about the over-reliance on particular orthodoxies in software packages, they are a significant part of a repertoire of tools that can aid analysis in ethnography and qualitative research more generally. They do not have to be used without criticality or an appreciation of their limits as well as their strengths. Gibbs (2014, 2018) has argued that while CAQDAS is not an analytical method in its own right, it has had an impact on the ways in which we might go about the analytic task. Of particular significance to ethnography is the increased capacity that software offers for the integration of data of different forms and in different modes (for example, audio, visual, digital, web sources, social media and geographical information), as well as assisting with the management of large amounts of complex data.

● KEY POINTS

- In ethnography, data analysis is an integral part of the research process. Our approach to analysis should be systematic, rigorous, flexible and imaginative. Analysis is to 'think with' as well as 'think about' data.
- Good data management will aid analysis. Data should be organized and stored in ways that facilitate retrieval, manipulation and display.
- Thematic analysis is a primary way of working with ethnographic data. Data are coded and categorized in order to identify themes and patterns as well as irregularities. Code-and-retrieve describes the process of attaching codes to data in order to group together and retrieve data.
- Ethnographic interviews, conversations and spoken interactions in the field can be analyzed in ways that pay particular attention to language. Approaches include narrative analysis, metaphorical analysis and domain analysis.

- Theorizing is a key aspect of analysis in ethnography. Theory refers to the generation and application of ideas. Abductive reasoning provides a framework for approaching theorization and generalization in ethnography.
- Computer software is widely available to support qualitative data analysis. This can help with data management, retrieval and display, and can be used to explore relationships between data. Software applications should be used reflexively.

■ FURTHER READING

Coffey, A. and Atkinson, P. (1996) *Making Sense of Qualitative Data: Complementary Research Strategies*. Thousand Oaks, CA: Sage.

Silver, C. and Lewins, A. (2014) *Using Software in Qualitative Research*, 2nd ed. London: Sage.

Silverman, D. (2015) *Interpreting Qualitative Data*, 5th ed. London: Sage.

CHAPTER SEVEN

REPRESENTATION AND THE WRITING OF ETHNOGRAPHY

CONTENTS

OBJECTIVES

After reading this chapter, you will:

- understand the ways in which ethnography is an authorial process;
- be able to describe the main elements and literary devices of a conventional ethnographic text;
- have an awareness of some of the critiques and debates in relation to ethnographic representation;
- be able to identify a range of 'alternative' ways of writing ethnography; and
- have an appreciation of some of the ways in which visual media can be used to support ethnographic representation.

ETHNOGRAPHY AS PRODUCTION

Ethnography encompasses a set of methods of inquiry for facilitating the understanding of social life. A key aspect of this ethnographic work is to present data and analyses in ways that represent (or perhaps more accurately re-present) the field sites and social actors with which we have engaged and studied. Ethnography is a term that describes not only the process of 'doing' ethnographic research (of being 'in the field'), but also the product of that research. The 'ethnography' is, thus, an artefact of ethnographic endeavour; a scholarly output in which and through which research is written up and, in turn received and 'read'. And, as data collection and data analysis are interwoven in ethnographic research, so too it is difficult to separate the tasks of analysis from the practical accomplishment of writing and of ethnographic production more generally. It is through our writing and production practices that we create ethnographic, analytical accounts of everyday social and cultural life. We draw on our data and interpretation to illustrate and substantiate our accounts. Ethnographic data and analyses come to life in the 'writing', as we seek to re-construct and re-present our observations and conversations in and through literary, usually (but not always) textual forms. It is important to note here that the writing (up) in ethnography is not just about conveying analysis, argument and conclusions to an audience or audiences, important though that may be. Writing, and more broadly representation and production practices in ethnography, is a crucial aspect of the research process itself. Writing ethnography is not simply a pragmatic task that occurs at or towards the end of research; nor is writing something that is undertaken in isolation from, or without recourse to, reflexive practices that underpin ethnographic research. Rather, writing is an integral part of how ethnography is done and gets done. As noted elsewhere in this volume, when ethnography is chosen as a method of inquiry, there are a range of decisions to be made in relation to both data collection and analytical strategy. Ethnographic data come in a variety of forms and can be subjected to a variety of analytical strategies (Coffey and Atkinson, 1996). Similarly, there are decisions to be taken as to how best to write about or represent ethnographic research. While the process of writing ethnographic research has never been static or monolithic in practice, there has been increasing recognition that there are genuine choices in relation to the conventions of writing and authorship in ethnography. Indeed, social scientists in general, and ethnographic scholars in particular, have become increasingly aware of and self-conscious about their writing practices (Becker, 2007; Van Maanen, 2011). There has been considerable reflection and challenge, with significant attention paid to the writing and reading of ethnographic texts. Developments in recent years have called into question what might have been perceived as taken-for-granted ethnographic writing practices, questioning assumptions about authorship and audience, and raising awareness of methodological choices in relation to ethnographic representation. In the course of this chapter some of the variety of textual and other forms of ethnographic production are introduced and described.

THE WRITING OF ETHNOGRAPHY

The act of writing is vital to ethnographic research; indeed ethnography has always been a literary endeavour. An outcome of ethnographic research is 'the ethnography' – and the conventional wisdom is that this is a scholarly written text through which the research is 'told' and comes to be understood. It is important that ethnographic writing and production are approached in the same way as ethnographic data collection and analysis – with thought, care, discipline and reflexivity. The writing (up) of ethnography is not just about committing words to the page; it is also about developing an awareness and an appreciation of writing as part of the craft work of ethnography. The 'crafting' of the text is central to the work of ethnography – there is the application of craft and skill in relation to the ways in which words are placed on the page, drawing on literary and textual conventions. Moreover, how ethnographic research is written up will determine how social worlds and social actors are represented, and come to be understood through that research.

The ethnographic monograph has been the classical way of writing up and sharing the endeavours of ethnographic fieldwork. The traditional ethnographic text is a conventional artefact, in that it is produced following a set of literary conventions. Angrosino (2007) identified the ways in which scholarly writing usually has a number of key elements that tend to follow a chronological order (see also Berg, 2004). Angrosino carried forward the assumption that an ethnographic report will have similar elements and follow similar principles. Thus, according to Angrosino, a conventional ethnographic text might be expected to have:

- A title – which describes the report simply and straightforwardly.
- An abstract or preface – giving a brief overview of the findings, method and structure of the report.
- An introduction – to provide an orientation to the reader, perhaps introducing the main research questions and key issues to be discussed.
- A review of the literature – providing a framework for the study, in relation to substantive, methodological and theoretical published work.
- A methodological review – describing methodological decisions and the processes of research design, data collection and data analysis, as well as perhaps providing a description of the research setting and participants.
- A report of findings or results – detailing the main outcomes of the research in relation to, and contextualized by, the research questions and the methodological/ substantive/theoretical framing already described.
- A conclusion – summarizing the main findings and key contribution, perhaps suggesting future research directions.
- References, notes and appendices – a range of materials which supplement the main text.

Such principles for the production of a scientific paper are, of course, helpful in providing a framework for organizing a written draft. However, they do not convey much about the processes of authorship nor the literary styles which ethnographers might use to convey meaning. Angrosino (2007, p. 79) himself acknowledged that 'the traditional scientific style of writing has always been something of a straitjacket for the ethnographer' and indicated that in recent years ethnographers have gradually found release from the confines of 'strict scientific writing'. But that rather underestimates the range of subtle ways in which ethnographers have always drawn on diverse literary devices to produce their scholarly, scientific, ethnographic texts.

Many written ethnographies do share common characteristics, and are constructed in particular ways in order to convey meaning based on close fieldwork and researcher engagement. For example, ethnographic authors have come to rely on detailed, 'thick' description (Geertz, 1973) in order to describe social and cultural worlds; writing that draws on close observation and has density and intensity that enables rich pictures to be painted with and through words. This usually means drawing on and sharing field notes, often including direct quotes from participants in the field. Of course, such descriptions are the result themselves of interpretation and are as 'seen' through the ethnographer's gaze. Nonetheless, there has been an implicit assumption that these detailed and contextualized descriptions of the small-scale and the local can and do convey the actual, contextualized experiences and perspectives of social actors from and in the field; and thus in turn are able to contribute to broader interpretations and understandings that go beyond the particular cases being described.

In transforming data and analyses into written ethnographic form there is skill at work – as we move from observer–researcher through to interpreter–analyst and on to being a writer–author. It is not necessary nor desirable to faithfully reproduce all field notes or all interview transcripts as part of the ethnographic text – as though they were able to reproduce some kind of 'true' picture. Indeed, without interpretation and the work of authorship, such an approach would actually produce at best a rather unwieldy or incoherent picture. Moreover, to reproduce field notes or interviews as though they were somehow objective, untainted by the researcher, is to misunderstand ethnographic practice. Indeed ethnographic field notes and interview texts are themselves produced and (co-)constructed; 'created' and 'written' by the ethnographer. Hence, the task of the ethnographic author is not to 'reproduce' but rather to 'represent', drawing on data and analyses to craft an authoritative account of the field – to tell a persuasive story. This implies an active authorship on the part of the ethnographer, who must make decisions on what and how to tell, based on their fieldwork experiences, data interpretations and literary style. It also suggests that it is difficult to separate the 'ethnography' from the 'ethnographer'. There is a balance to be struck, of course, between describing the setting or topic of study and ensuring the ethnographer's presence in the field is appropriately and reflexively acknowledged in the written text. While convention would suggest that the emphasis should be on the former, it is important that we recognize that it is the ethnographer who is tasked with description, and through which interpretation and writing flow. As Davies (2008, p. 255) notes,

In analysis and writing, ethnographers move between their interpretations on others' constructions of reality, their own creation of new constructions and their expression of these evolving understandings in yet another, usually written, form. This final written product is a mediation that is itself a conduit for further mediations, in particular between author and various possible audiences.

Ethnographic monographs, like all other forms of writing (both scholarly writing such as journal articles, but also fictional writing and storytelling) draw on a range of literary conventions and rhetorical devices to create plausible and coherent accounts of social and cultural life. Over the past three decades or more there has been a growing interest in how such conventions and devices are used in ethnographic writing in order to create recognizable and believable representations – what Davies refers to as 'textualization' (2008, p. 256). Thus, there is a transformative process at work in the writing of ethnography, in moving from a 'field' and field notes to another kind of 'text'; we draw on a variety of techniques and ways of writing to undertake that task. Atkinson (1992) referred to the inherent intertextuality of ethnographic reportage; that is, to the ways in which an ethnographic product brings together various texts (for example, field notes, interview transcripts, documents collected from the field, materials produced during fieldwork, as well as previously published work), in dialogue and through interpretation. There has also been attention to genre in ethnographic writing; to the ways in which ethnographic accounts are structured in order to draw in and persuade the reader. It is important, of course, to have an awareness of the audiences for which we are writing and how our texts will be read. We write with an implied readership in mind and will want our audiences to be persuaded by the strength of our arguments. Thus the ways in which we choose to convey meaning through our textual practices and genre will be in relation to what we are wanting to convey (i.e. what story or stories we are telling), how we feel our writing will be received by our readers, and how audiences will be persuaded that this is a serious and authoritative account.

There are a number of parallels between various kinds of literary writing and ethnography. Indeed ethnography has historically drawn upon and continues to draw upon (and indeed influence) a wide range of literary styles. This includes travel writing (see Richardson and Lockridge, 2004), journalism (see Hermann, 2016, for a recent account of ethnographic journalism) and fiction (see Jacobson and Larsen, 2014; Narayan, 1999). Richardson (1990) has noted that the narrative form provides a powerful vehicle through which everyday life and ethnography can be organized; both are concerned with creating structure and order, through which everyday experiences and events are played out and come to be understood. Language, through its many qualities, both creates value and gives meaning. Thus, narrative genres provide recognized structures and patterns through which the mundane and ordinary, as well as the extraordinary are routinely and culturally understood. In similar vein, Van Maanen (2011) has explored the ways in which ethnographic writing has long drawn on the trope of the realist tale; that is, using tightly edited quotations and field observations to create a text that brings to the fore the words and experiences of people being studied, through a silent authorial voice that is dominant almost by its invisibility. In realist tales, the author is an absent presence; what are foregrounded and made explicit are the 'voices' and 'tales' of the social actors of the setting, whose stories are being 'told'. Thus the account is presented as if it were 'real' or 'true' in some absolute sense, and the ethnographer (as author) is really 'just' a vehicle through which the account emerges and is seen. Of course realist 'tales' are just that, carefully constructed and ethnographer-mediated tales; created accounts where the absence of the author is purposeful and meant. As Van Maanen argues, 'a realist tale offers one reading and culls the facts carefully to support that reading. Little can be discovered in such texts that has not been put there by the fieldworker as a way of supporting a particular interpretation' (1988, p. 53). Ethnographic texts, of all kinds, are created and authored; they are made (up).

RETHINKING ETHNOGRAPHIC REPRESENTATION

Since the 1980s there has been considerable critical attention paid to the writing of ethnography, and in particular to its textual conventions and authorial voice. While it is still the case that most ethnographic texts continue to follow the conventional format of the scholarly monograph or academic journal paper, there has been a heightened awareness of some of the problematics involved in representing culture. Moreover, there has been an increasing recognition that there are choices to be made in how ethnography gets written. We can choose how we write about, for and with our participants. Alongside debate and critique in relation to ethnographic writing, there has been a growth in awareness of variety in ethnographic representation. With this have come opportunities to practise new ways of producing ethnographic texts, a key aspect of which has been the increased recognition that 'in all ethnographies … there are a variety of voices in the text: some of them the voices of informants, others the different voices of the ethnographer, who may speak, for example, as interlocutor, social actor or analyst' (Davies, 2008, p. 263).

The scrutiny that has been given to ethnographic writing and texts emerged from, and has been influenced by, postmodern debates across a number of disciplines, concerned with vexed issues of cultural representation and the textual construction of polyvocal realities. In social anthropology, the edited collection *Writing Culture: The Poetics and Politics of Ethnography* (Clifford and Marcus, 1986), is often identified as an important watershed in problematizing the taken-for-granted textual conventions and authorial authority of ethnographic texts. This collection called for greater reflexivity in ethnographic writing, prompted a more self-conscious approach to writing practice and spoke to more innovative and dialogic approaches to ethnographic representation. Framed through postmodern sensibilities, the claims to authenticity that are implicit in ethnographic work that adopts a dominant perspective (most usually that of the ethnographer as objective or neutral observer and author) were rendered uncertain and open to question.

Some commentators have referred to the critique of ethnographic writing and authorship as a 'crisis of representation', constituting a 'profound rupture' whereby the 'erosion of classic norms in anthropology (objectivism, complicity with colonialism, social life structured by fixed rituals and customs, ethnographies as monuments to a culture) was complete' (Denzin and Lincoln, 2005, p. 18). Others have questioned the extent of this 'rupture', suggesting something approaching evolution rather than revolution. Woods (1996), for example, in sidelining postmodern or poststructural influences relatively early in these debates, suggested that reflexive approaches to text are but logical extensions to interactionist practice, and as such are transgressive rather than particularly progressive. Similarly, Spencer has made the point that 'many ethnographers in the generation of fieldworkers trained in the 1970s and early 1980s had simply ceased to believe in the models of scientific and textual authority provided by our disciplinary ancestors' (2001, p. 443). The debates that have ensued and the ways in which ethnographic writing has taken on a variety of forms, serve to reinforce the view that writing should be afforded the same reflexive approach as other aspects of ethnographic research practice.

There have been a number of wider influences that have been brought to bear in thinking about authorship and authority in ethnography. This includes an intellectual movement associated with the so-called 'rediscovery of rhetoric' (Atkinson and Coffey, 1995). This philosophical movement, speaking from and to a range of disciplines across the humanities and social sciences, as well as physical and biological sciences, brings into relief the centrality of rhetoric to all scholarly work concerned with argument and persuasion; this readily includes ethnography as a scholarly text designed to tell a plausible account of social life and social worlds. The 'rediscovery of rhetoric' brings to the fore the 'conventional' separation of rhetoric and science, along with their attendant commitments. On the one hand there is the rhetorical, through which opinion is given and persuasion enacted. On the other hand there is scientific logic, method and evidence that serve to consign rhetoric to the very margins of legitimate scholarship. It could well be argued that the aspirations of modern ethnography were rooted in the possibility of being 'scientific' – that is based on 'objective' evidence, and reporting through a scientific language of 'neutral' observation. The 'rediscovery' that rhetorical devices are central to all scholarly work, including the physical and biological sciences, has had an impact on how knowledge is conceptualized within and across a range of disciplines. For example, it has become clear that even the most scientific texts and reports of hard 'science' are accounts which contain many rhetorical features, designed precisely to persuade the reader of the 'objectivity' of the science (Lynch and Wolgar, 1990). Moreover, the distinction between scientific fact and textual production has come to be seen as at best unhelpful. All 'scientific' texts are produced to serve particular purposes, and there are no texts that are necessarily more authentic or 'scientific' than any other. All scholarly work draws on literary devices and ways of telling in order to construct narratives of authenticity and authority. In questioning the authenticity or assumed dominance of some textual forms over others there is then, by definition, an opening up of alternative textual possibilities. For ethnography practice, this has meant an explicit recognition of the conventions that are used in its textual production, and therefore an opening up of new ways of writing about and representing social worlds.

This 'permission' to utilize different textual arrangements to those which are conventional; and the recognition of the importance of rhetoric in 'doing' and accounting for science, can be seen alongside sustained and particular ideological critiques of ethnography and its textual products. Said (1978), for example, elucidated a powerful commentary on the orientalism of Western observation, implying that ethnographic texts are both privileged and privileging. More generally, postcolonial commentators have argued that the authority of the ethnographer has been maintained through various exploitative texts of description and classification (see, for example, Marcus, 1992; Minh-ha, 2000). Others have pointed to the not insignificant challenges of undertaking postcolonial ethnographies which speak to variable experiences of contemporary globalization (Comaroff and Comaroff, 2003). Postcolonial critiques of ethnography are not limited to what might be perceived as sustained observation and writing of the exotic 'other'. As Fordham noted in relation to her school ethnography in her native North America: 'Those empowered to use one of society's most powerful weapons – the pen – can permanently shape or transform our thinking ... our perceptions of an entire generation could be permanently altered as a result of these ethnographic images' (1996, p. 341).

Feminist scholars have also paid attention to the possibilities and problematics of the ethnographic text, identifying and challenging similar issues of dominance and privilege. In a sustained dialogue between ethnography and feminism, representation has been a key point of departure (Clough, 1992; Wolf, 1992). Stacey (1988), in a relatively early discussion on the possibilities for a feminist ethnography, raised concerns in relation to ethnographic production. Describing ethnography as ironic for feminism, Stacey noted that there are real risks of exploitation and betrayal in ethnographic work and its textual products. In a more recent paper on the imperatives for a feminist ethnography, Schrock (2013) reiterates the important point that ethnographic representations are not value-free, and may have consequences for those who are being written about and represented. This is a rearticulation of the argument that conventional ethnographic texts may serve to disguise exploitative processes (Clough, 1992), with the possibility that the 'observed' are silenced, and (only) rendered visible and audible through the observations and texts of the ethnographer.

This critical attention that has been paid to ethnographic texts, both in relation to the conventions that are used and the messages that are transmitted, has an impact on the ways in which we think about and conceptualize ethnographic practice and representation. In very general terms, a more self-conscious and reflexive approach to the practice of ethnographic writing has developed. Writing is no longer, if indeed it ever was, a taken-for-granted aspect of the ethnographic endeavour. There is a greater appreciation that writing is an important part of what it is to undertake reflexive ethnography. We have become more aware that we draw on a range of literary conventions in our writing, and that these conventions are used with purpose precisely because they enable us to write accounts that 'appear' authentic, plausible and authoritative. Thus there is recognition that ethnographic authorship is purposive; ethnographies are authored in ways that render them believable and with particular stories to tell. Thus, there should be an understanding that there are other stories to tell and different ways of telling. As with other authors, ethnographers have choice in relation to genre and style. We have also become much more aware of the power dimensions of ethnographic research which can be encapsulated through our writing practices and textual products. Over recent decades therefore, there has also been an opening up of the possibilities of ethnographic texts, what they are and what they might be.

OTHER WAYS OF 'WRITING' ETHNOGRAPHY

While the conventional scholarly ethnographic monograph is still used extensively as a mode through which to produce an *ethnography*, such a strategy must be considered self-consciously and not simply by default, as though such conventional formats are somehow neutral or devoid of authorship. We must be thoughtful in the ways in which we render some stories more prominently than others, and reflexive in acknowledging the authorial voice. Alongside such ethnographically conventional styles and formats, has been an aesthetic move towards a variety of different representation styles. These have included the use of poetry, drama and fiction in ethnography. These creative, and differently 'conventional' ways of writing ethnography respond, in part at least, to the critiques of conventional ethnographic texts; adopting styles of writing that are different to the scholarly textual form can promote a more reflexive and self-conscious attention to ethnographic authorship. Even if these possibilities are considered and then rejected, they have purpose in alerting us to the active process of writing and in prompting us to articulate what it is we want our ethnographic texts to convey.

These 'alternative' ways of writing can be located within what some commentators have called a textual turn within ethnography, and indeed within qualitative research more generally (Ellis and Bochner, 1996). There has been considerable debate about how widely these different forms of representation are used in ethnography, or indeed whether they should be used at all to write scholarly work. Some have suggested that alternative forms of representing research, which perhaps transcend or reject 'traditional' scientific convention, can capture the imagination of non-academic audiences in particular. Of course, such 'troubling' writing practices can equally serve as counterproductive to those more used to or expecting a conventional scientific report (see Atkinson et al., 2003. Other commentators have raised concerns about whether such approaches actually address the issues of power and authority in ethnography. Lather (1991, 2001), for example, has argued that alternative modes of representation do not necessarily remove issues of power from ethnographic texts, and are also at risk of falling into static claims of authenticity. Furthermore, self-conscious and creative texts can also risk aestheticizing social life, focusing on the writing rather than the social phenomena under consideration, and indeed introducing new ways of privileging the author (not just as ethnographer but also as poet, writer of prose, fiction writer, playwright and so forth). However, such approaches can usefully be considered as part of the ethnographic repertoire, and can provide alternative ways of writing ethnography. Below are brief descriptions of some different approaches to the production of an ethnographic 'text'.

Dialogic approaches to producing ethnography: ethnodrama and ethnotheatre

Texts which follow the conventions of the theatre or cinema, and which take a dialogic approach to ethnographic writing, can transform data and interpretation into scripts and performance. Such approaches draw on the dramaturgical turn, and on the concept of the performativity of everyday life. Supporters of ethnodrama and ethnotheatre argue that such representations have the capacity to promote multi-vocal, multiple and layered versions of complex social worlds and events. Examples include Bluebond-Langer's dramaturgical approach to exploring the social worlds of dying children (1980) and Fox's multi-voiced text to re-present contested voices of sexual offences (1996). Saldaña's edited collection gives a good overview and extension of this arts-based ethnographic research practice, showing how theatre and ethnography can be compatible and mutually supportive (2005). Mienczakowski (1995, 1996, 1999) has used theatrical re-performance in a variety of social work settings, arguing that performed ethnography can make research more accessible to a variety of audiences, including informants. As a supporter and practitioner of ethnodrama, Mienczakowski (2001) also observes some of the tensions of performed research; while designed to empower informants he acknowledges that ethnodrama can also expose them, potentially placing informants and vulnerable audiences at risk.

Poetry and prose: ethnopoetry

Ethnographic poems draw on poetic literary conventions including prose, rhythm, rhyme and tempo to write and represent ethnographic research. Poetry can be an evocative and potentially powerful mode of writing, delivery and performance. Ethnographers have used poetry to share their data and analyses, as well as their own experiences of fieldwork. Bloor's 'Rime of the globalised mariner' (2013) provides an exemplar of the genre in action. In fact, Bloor reminds his readers that the sociologist C. Wright Mills called for sociological poetry in the 1940s, 'as a style of experience and expression that reports social facts and at the same time reveals their human meaning' (see Mills, 2008, p. 34). (See also Marechal and Linstead, 2010, who show how attention to poetic technique and craft skills can be ethnographically fruitful.) Richardson argued that ethnographic poetry sits in contrast to the 'constraining belief that the purpose of a social science text is to convey information as facts or themes or notions existing independent of the contexts in which they were found or produced – as if the story we have recorded, transcribed, edited and written up in prose snippets is the one and only true one' (2000, p. 933).

Storytelling: ethnographic fiction

It is something of a misnomer to conceptualize ethnography according to a strict distinction of 'fiction' and 'non-fiction'. There might be any number of reasons why a setting, or people from that setting, might be fictionally represented in some way in ethnographic texts. Indeed most, if not all ethnographic writing, will involve elements of fiction, almost as a matter of course, and with no intention to 'deceive' or pass as 'fictional'. Fiction in ethnography might include representing some people or places fictionally; for example, changing the names of informants or settings, describing composite characters, and using hypothetical or composite events. Such practices might be done for ethical reasons, perhaps to protect identities or manage particular sensitivities in the field. Fiction can, somewhat ironically, be a matter of research ethics, used with purpose to disguise people or places to ensure they are not put at risk or are easily identified by the research. Equally, it is usual in ethnographic writing to operate with a form of literary license, in condensing and attempting to make sense of a setting within what is always a limited word length. In ethnographic texts we routinely juxtapose and reorder actions, talk and other data extracts for literary effect. Fiction has also be used explicitly and purposively, using various fictional genres to tell an ethnographically informed story which is grounded in, but not limited to data and fieldwork experience. The volume edited by Banks and Banks (1998) provides a range of examples of ethnographic fiction, also showing the ways in which fiction and/in ethnography has a long history (Atkinson, 1990). Other examples of ethnographic fiction, clearly identified as such, include Angrosino (1998), who translated ethnographic data from mental health settings into a series of short stories, and the ethnographic novel *After Life* by Hecht (2006).

Autoethnography: writing selves

Autoethnography is a particular form of ethnographic practice which draws on the researcher's own personal experiences as a platform for analysis and writing, and for understanding social and cultural life more generally. As well as a process, autoethnography produces a 'product' – an autoethnography (Ellis et al., 2011). Often deeply evocative, such writings can include a range of genres and styles – narrative, prose, poetry, fiction, dialogic scripts and metaphor – and have often been used to tell of and write about deeply personal and sensitive events – for example, sexual abuse, mental health issues, abortion, personal relationships and bereavement. Some practitioners of the genre have also turned autoethnographic texts into performance pieces of ethnotheatre. There have been robust debates within qualitative research in relation to autoethnography and the complex (and some would argue uncomfortable) relationships between ethnography, biography and therapy (see Reed-Danahay, 2001; Holman Jones, 2005). Ellis and Bochner, who have been pivotal in the development of autoethnography, have suggested that ethnographic writing can be practised in this context 'as a form of creative nonfiction, to take certain expressive liberties associated with the arts, but to feel the ethical pull of converting data into experiences readers can use', as well as for reaching wider audiences: 'not only to write *about* families, organizations, communities and institutions, but also to write *to* them as well' (1996, p. 28). Examples of autoethnography include Paget (1990, 1993) on living with cancer and Lahman (2008) on the end of a pregnancy; also see Ellis (2004) for a methodological novel on conducting and writing autoethnography.

These varied examples of (re)writing ethnography using different styles of writing all serve to illustrate the more general point; that ethnographic texts are composed, authored, written and made. Moreover, there are choices in relation to the production of the ethnography. There are a variety of ways of giving structure and shape to ethnographic writing, drawing on alternative and varied literary conventions. The choice will involve thinking about which style or genre might best suit the aims of the written piece and the audience that you have in mind or are required to write for. Opening up the possibilities of alternative ways of writing ethnography, even if the decision is to adopt a straightforward 'conventional' journal article, helps to foreground the important point that ethnographers are authors of the stories they choose to tell.

WAYS OF SEEING: BEYOND WRITING

The ways in which we represent ethnographic data and analyses are, of course, not confined to 'written' texts. Indeed, ethnography has always been open to working with and across different modes of expression. For example, there is a long history of ethnographic film documentary, cinematography and photography (see Ball and Smith, 2001; also see Becker, 1995). Visual methods can be incorporated into ethnographic research at a number of points in the research process: from data collected in visual form – still and moving images, pictures, drawings and other artefacts – through to data analysis and research outputs. Visual methods can be used to display and interrogate ethnographic data, drawing out new meanings through creative visual means. Miles and Huberman (1994) made a good case for utilizing a wide range of visual tools for displaying qualitative data, both in ways which aid the analytic process, and for showing the outcomes of analysis. These visual tools might include the use of diagrams, charts, graphs and matrices to provide new ways of organizing and thinking about textual data collected during fieldwork. Such visualization can be used to simplify and codify data, as well as for illustrating order, pattern and relationship in and between data. In simple terms, Miles and Huberman emphasized that such visual 'representational' devices can be used heuristically during data analysis as well as being included in ethnographic texts to provide illustration. As such, these become tools through which textual data come to be interrogated and differently displayed, rather than becoming the definitive outcome or report of research. That is, they are supplemental to, as well as illustrative of, ethnographic writing in textual form. They do not replace the conventional written text.

There are other ways in which visual media and modes can be used to complement or indeed replace textual ethnographic representation. For example, still and moving film production in ethnography has been traditionally used to do particular kinds of reportage. Ethnographic documentary has been most readily associated with social anthropological explorations of other cultures. There is a long history of film, using both photography and cinematography as part of the realist tradition of ethnography. Emerging out of the documentary traditions of the late nineteenth and early twentieth centuries, such practices have much in common with the ethnographic text. As Ball and Smith note, the 'realist impulse' in documentary is 'paramount'; documentary film is distinguishable from fictional film, in that it is about reportage rather than invention. However, 'documentary is also designed to encourage viewers to come to a particular conclusion about how the world is and the way it works, much as occurs in ethnographic texts' (2001, p. 304). Conventional social anthropological documentary from this perspective is 'composed' and 'made', in just the same way as other forms of ethnographic representation, and thus can and indeed has been subject to the same kinds of scholarly scrutiny as conventional authoritative ethnographic works (particularly in relation to postcolonial critique of eroticizing and othering different cultures and practices).

Visual methods in the social sciences, as well as filmic technologies, have moved on considerably in recent years. While still and moving images have almost always formed part of the ethnographic repertoire, there has not been universal adoption. Visual anthropologists working with visual media have focused more on moving images, while visual sociologists have tended towards photography. Anthropologists have 'always' included documentary film of a high technical standard, often with audiences in mind beyond the academy. However, Becker's note almost four decades ago that, 'visual social science isn't something brand new … but it might as well be' (1979, p. 7), still has contemporary resonance. In many areas of social science, including ethnographic methods, visual methods are still considered to be relatively new and innovative, and often serve as an adjunct to, rather than a replacement for the written text. Yet visual ways of presenting ethnographic data and analyses can be considered in similar ways to other representational forms – for example, poetry, theatrical scripts or performance – with the capacity to provide alternative, perhaps more polyvocal and multiple ways, of showing data and ideas. In articulating a case for visual ethnography, Pink suggests that images have the potential to both generate and represent new forms of ethnographic knowledge, challenging the view that the written word is 'essentially a superior medium of ethnographic representation', and that there is and should not be 'a hierarchy of knowledge or media for ethnographic representation' (2013, p. 10).

In the not so distant past, film making was a relatively specialist genre, requiring both professional knowledge and technical resources. The contemporary techno-logical and digital landscape makes film recording and visual production much more accessible for ethnographers, and indeed social researchers more generally. It is now easier than it has ever been for the ethnographic researcher to produce high-quality photographic and other visual material using everyday devices and knowledges. Like film, still photographs have a long association with ethnogra-phy, and have long been used for illustrative purposes in ethnographic writings. Photographs can be used to gather and display data, and can be productive means of co-producing forms of representation with research participants. Mobile devices, such as phones and tablets, make in situ photography easier and more accessible than it has ever been. Ethnographers, as well as publishers, have become more willing and accustomed to including images within academic writing. However, it remains the case that images are not universally used in ethnographic production, and where they are used they still tend to form a small aside in what are otherwise predominantly word-based narratives. Pink (2013) provides a range of examples for disrupting this dominant association between words and pictures in contemporary ethnography, and shows the ways in which visual methods can be used to create alternative ethnographic texts.

Where research is undertaken in material settings, and where ethnographic data might include material artefacts and objects, data display and ethnographic representa-tion can go further still. For example, ethnographic outputs can include public displays and exhibitions, which might contain a mixture of text, images and things. The devel-opment of information technologies and the web also provides yet further possibilities for data display and data linking, as well as the opportunity to reach different audiences with ethnographic outputs. For example, hypermedia has been shown to be a platform for approaching ethnographic writing in non-linear and multifaceted ways, providing opportunities to include a range of different modes of data and analysis within a single mediated online structure, with the possibilities of new semiotic forms and meanings to be made and displayed (Dicks et al., 2005; Pink, 2013).

In this chapter I have been keen to show that there are options in respect of writing and representation in ethnography. In just the same way as we make principled decisions about the processes of data collection and data analysis, so too there must be an awareness of choices we have and make, consciously or unconsciously, about our textual practices. An awareness of the variety of forms of ethnographic representation is not, though, an unprincipled invitation to experimentation without purpose. Writing and representation are ways in which we 'do' ethnography as well as produce ethnography, and come with authorial responsibilities. It is important that, as ethnographers, we appreciate the ways in which our writing practices represent and re-present social settings, and provide opportunities documenting multiple realities of the field.

KEY POINTS

- Writing and authorship are key aspects of ethnographic research practice. Writing is an integral part of how ethnography is done and gets done. 'Ethnographies' are produced and written.

- The 'ethnography' is a scholarly output in which and through which ethnographic data and analyses are shared. The 'conventional' way of writing an ethnography draws on a stock of literary devices in order to provide an authoritative account. Much ethnographic writing draws on the trope of the realist tale, using tightly edited quotations and field observations to create a text that foregrounds the words and experiences of people being studied. In realist tales, the author is an 'absent presence', and portrayed as a neutral observer of social life.

- There have been postcolonial, feminist and other postmodern critiques of ethnographic writing. These have questioned authority and authorship, and raised issues of power and domination in relation to ethnographic representation practices. For some, such critique has been seen as a rupture or crisis. For others, a reflexive approach to writing and representing ethnography is a natural extension of interpretive practice.

- Alternative genres have been proposed that enable more multi-layered, polyvocal and self-conscious ethnographic texts to be produced. These include poetry, performance, theatrical scripts, fiction and autoethnography.

- Film and photography has a long history in ethnography, with the documentary being a classic ethnographic form. Visual methods can be used to display data and create ethnographic texts. These provide opportunities to disrupt conventional textual approaches and offer opportunities for co-production. Like other representational modes, visual methods should be used reflexively and self-consciously.

■ FURTHER READING

Gay y Blason, P. and Wardle, H. (2007) *How to Read Ethnography.* Abingdon, Oxon and New York: Routledge.

Goodall, H. (2000) *Writing the New Ethnography.* Walnut Creek, CA: AltaMira Press.

Van Maanen, J. (2011). *Tales of the Field: On Writing Ethnography*, 2nd ed. Chicago: The University of Chicago Press.

CHAPTER EIGHT

THE FUTURE(S) OF ETHNOGRAPHY

CONTENTS

OBJECTIVES

After reading this chapter, you will:

- be able to articulate some of the ways in which ethnography has changed, and some of the characteristics that have endured;
- be able to identify and describe the challenges and possibilities presented to ethnography by technological advancement; and
- have an understanding of some of the ways in which ethnography might develop in the future.

THE MOMENTS OF ETHNOGRAPHY

Ethnography has a long and varied history. Originally grounded in the nineteenth and early twentieth century fieldwork practices of social anthropology, it has since been practised within, benefited from and been influenced by a variety of perspectives and disciplines. And ethnography has not stood still over the course of this historical trajectory of a hundred years or more. Denzin and Lincoln (2011) have provided a very particular historical narrative of ethnography, and of qualitative research more generally, describing its development as a series of 'moments', of which so far there have been nine (and counting). Through these historical moments (or phases) ethnography is located within the methodological and epistemological contexts of the time – from an objectivist and positivist programme of the early twentieth century, through various periods of modernism (where attempts were made to codify and formalize qualitative methods), and on towards a multiplicity of perspective and a diversification of approach encapsulated in the 1970s and early 1980s. Denzin and Lincoln's historization captures the opportunities afforded by ethnography, as well as challenges that have been faced, particularly to its textual practices, as personified by the so-called crisis of representation (see Chapter 7, this volume). Their account also identifies considerable and fast-paced change over the last 30 years or so, from 'the postmodern period of experimental ethnographic writing' (Denzin and Lincoln, 2000, p. 17) symbolizing continuing tensions and diversity; through to the later 1990s where there was a 'cacophony of voices speaking with various agendas' (Denzin and Lincoln 1994, p. 409); and on towards what they describe as the 'seventh moment' of ferment and explosion, of breaks from the past, of critical conversation, and with a focus on previously silenced voices. Denzin and Lincoln identify the eighth and present moment as symbolized by yet more ruptions and the rise of evidenced-based practice, situated in the context of both a changing world and an increasingly sophisticated theoretical and methodological landscape within which contemporary interpretist work is situated. The ninth moment represents the future of qualitative inquiry and ethnographic practice. Denzin and Lincoln thus define qualitative research in relation to 'a series of tensions, contradictions and hesitations' (2011, p. 15), while holding fast to a belief that 'critical qualitative inquiry inspired by the sociological imagination can make the world a better place' (Denzin and Lincoln, 2011, p. xii).

This historical conceptualization of ethnography is often used as a reference point in relation to ethnography's pasts, presents and futures, though it has been the subject of some criticism. Denzin and Lincoln present a rather linear and perhaps too fixed a view of what some commentators see as a more messy ethnographic reality; criticism has also focused on the privileging of the recent past and present as being the periods of the most significant and dramatic changes (see Atkinson et al., 2001 for an overview). Others have noted that this temporal understanding of ethnography is based on the development of qualitative research in Anglo-Saxon areas; for example, alternative views of the development of qualitative methods are available through tracing their journey in German-speaking areas (see Alasuutari, 2004; Flick, 2014). Indeed Denzin and Lincoln (2011) acknowledged these critiques, and have recognized that their take on the development of ethnography (and qualitative methods more generally) is a particular one. However, they still argue for its usefulness, not least in providing a framework through which to describe possible pasts, presents and imagined futures of ethnography.

In this chapter it is to the future of ethnography that attention is turned. There are three sets of factors that might usefully be identified in which and through which contemporary ethnographic research is practised. Firstly, and as Denzin and Lincoln (2011) acknowledge, the world has changed significantly, meaning there are new contexts in which ethnography must operate and through which ethnographic understanding is realized. Secondly, there have been a series of changes to the research environment in which all social inquiry takes place, with new imperatives to be navigated and addressed. Thirdly, there are continuing methodological and epistemological contexts within which and through which ethnographers continue to create, innovate and hone their craft.

NEW GLOBAL AND LOCAL CONTEXTS FOR ETHNOGRAPHY

It is clear that the world into which the late nineteenth and early twentieth century ethnographers travelled and researched was very different from our contemporary experiences of social and cultural life. Both global and hyper-local processes have refined and redefined our understandings and experiences of place and distance; ethnography, like any other commodity or cultural form, now travels and circulates on a global stage, while continuing to have the capacity to operate at the very local level. One consequence of this is that the distinction between ethnography 'at home' or 'away', is not as starkly drawn as it might once have been. Whether we are conducting ethnographic research 'at home' or 'away', in familiar institutions, organizations or communities on our doorstep, or much further afield, the experiences we are seeking to understand will now be located within, and shaped by, both local and global contexts and processes. This provides new possibilities and opportunities for ethnography, while also adding complication. It is possibly more rather than less difficult to identify a bounded field for study; for example, what we understand by community has changed – we can have hyper-global as well as local communities. It can be methodologically challenging to access and make sense of everyday experiences that are differently mediated – for example, in both online and offline fora. Globalization must be understood, at least in part, in relation to significant and still advancing digital and technological development. The ways in which people communicate and practise in everyday worlds have been, and continue to be, transformed by mobile and web technologies. Moreover, we now inhabit social worlds where everyday technologies of surveillance, and the routine digital recording of action and interaction, have become ever more present and normalized. With this come particular ethical and legal concerns (Lyon, 2001) of course, as well as challenges to the very nature and distinctiveness of ethnographic practice. As Denzin and Lincoln (2011) have observed, the very warranty of ethnographers to observe and study (and the 'ownership' of field notes and other recordings) might be seen to be at stake in ways that have thus far been unprecedented.

Of course, global technological development has changed the possibilities for ethnography in other ways. Many people, across the world, now live in and inhabit virtual worlds, and have expansive and extensive virtual and online networks. These range from genuinely global communities, where everyday interactions with people from across the world (who have never met, and probably will never meet face-to-face) are routine, through to hyper-local, real-time communities of practice – but where social media, instant messaging and shared online interactivity changes the ways in which local communities are 'made' and through which they communicate. There are opportunities now to undertake ethnographic research that is genuinely global, unbounded by a physical 'place'. There are also possibilities of studying newly formed and differently mediated hyper-local communities. Ethnographers are able to inhabit offline and online worlds, navigate those spaces that lie in between, and gather new forms of digitally mediated data.

The tools of the ethnographic trade have also been transformed. Mobile and other digital technologies are available globally and in increasingly accessible ways. They do not necessarily, nor indeed frequently, require specialist skills and knowledge, outside of the realms of our everyday practices. Indeed for many people across the world communicative and capturing technologies have become ubiquitous within daily practice. Sound, as well as moving and still images, can now be recorded and widely shared by mobile devices that are almost universally available and commonly used. People can be contacted instantaneously, and real-time conversations are now possible through a range of media. Information, in various different modes, can be shared with anyone, anywhere in the world, at little more than a touch of a button. Notes can be made, copied, edited and expanded with relative ease; text can readily be juxtaposed alongside images and sounds; photographs can be tagged with geographically precise location data and without the need for expensive or particularly specialist software.

Technology has the capacity to transform fieldwork and the experiences of ethnography. But it is important that we remain reflexive of these transformations, and embrace technology with a thoughtful criticality, according it the same level of reflexivity as other ethnographically mediated practices. Technology provides new ways of doing ethnography and of being an ethnographer, as well as opening up new fields for the investigation and understanding of everyday social life. At the same time, there is something to be said for not losing sight of the integrity of ethnography as embodied experience (Coffey, 1999). As Angrosino noted, participant observation has particular value in that we are able to immerse ourselves

in the ebb and flow, in the ambiguities of life as lived by real people … the more we fix this or that snapshot of that life and the more we have the capacity to disseminate … that image globally and instantaneously, the more we risk violating our sense of what makes real life so particular and so endlessly fascinating. (2007, p. 92)

A CHANGING RESEARCH CULTURE

In recent years, there has been an increasing emphasis on innovation in social research, alongside calls for research to be evidence based and impactful. An example of this drive comes from the UK, where in 2005 the Economic and Social Research Council (ESRC), one of the UK research councils funded by government, and through which significant science research funding is competitively allocated, established a National Centre for Research Methods (NCRM). This initiative had a specific aim of enhancing the social science research community's capacity to improve the quality and impact of research through the development of cutting edge methodological tools and techniques. The ambition was to design and implement 'a strategic research agenda that will facilitate methodological innovation in quantitative and qualitative research and their cross-fertilisation, ensuring that the UK is at the forefront of international developments in social research methodology' (ESRC, 2006, p. 25). The framing was in terms of a 'step change' in the quality and range of methodological skills, through the provision of an infrastructure for methodological innovation and excellence.

Innovation in relation to social research methods is a somewhat vexed issue. What might count as innovation in one methodological arena or in one discipline might already be routinely practised in another. For example, in relation to ethnography and qualitative methods more generally, it has been the very adoption of these approaches across a range of disciplines and fields that has been heralded as innovative in their time; while in social anthropology, for example, they have long been custom and practice ways of gathering data and generating understandings of social life. Similarly, the increased use of visual methods, helped by technological advances, has been represented as innovative practice in many arenas of social science, while at the same time visual images have long been part of the research repertoire of the humanities. And by definition 'successful' innovations stop being innovative over time, as they are 'mainstreamed' and accepted as good research practice. In fact, a case can be made that methodological innovation only really has affordance when it is no longer necessary to make claims to innovation, when 'new' methods and approaches become established as part of our everyday research repertoire.

Calls to methodological innovation have been widespread within ethnography and qualitative research more generally; not least, innovative practices are an integral part of the historization of qualitative research as advanced by Denzin and Lincoln (2011), where out of tensions, contestations and fragmentation come new ways of doing and representing research. A test of methodological innovation is in relation to its capacity to enhance and have benefit beyond what is already possible or achieved through existing and accepted research practices. Hence 'innovative' ethnographic research practice must be capable of both sustaining and enhancing what it is to 'do' ethnography, including its capacity to generate and advance understanding of social worlds, institutions, processes and lives. In ethnography, as in social research more generally, the benefits of innovating, enhancing or adapting can be multiple and varied. There are a number of different ways in which the perceived benefits of methodological innovation might be conceptualized and measured. For example, new ways of research practice might lead to:

- possibilities of collecting more or different data;
- opportunities of accessing new research settings or participants;
- greater efficiency, perhaps promoting a better use of research resources;
- greater impact, or the capacity to reach different audiences;
- deeper and more nuanced knowledge or understanding;
- richer, enhanced research relationships;
- improved ethical practice.

Such benefits of innovative research practice are not all about impact in any grand sense of the word, but they are about being clear regarding the purpose and wider mission of research. But perhaps innovation is the wrong word and the wrong agenda for ethnographic research. It is almost inconceivable that there are going to be wholly new methods for practising and producing ethnography – approaches that have not already been thought of and tried out in some form or another – to be invented, tested and released on to a waiting qualitative research community. Enhancement, adaptation and the sharing of creative practices seem more realistic ambitions, though such ambitions do not have the same cachet that the term innovation might have. To be innovative is to be cutting edge and ahead of one's time, risky even – in a good way. To develop, enhance or adapt suggests a much more pedestrian register – perhaps one of 'getting on' and perhaps just 'getting by', but can also include being responsive to new research contexts and challenges, and being prepared to change tack should new opportunities present themselves.

It is also important to recognize that methodological development is a process rather than an event; the capacity to adapt and to respond to circumstances and opportunities that arise is one of the markers of a good ethnographic project. Ethnography, by its very nature, is flexible and creative. Indeed, we might wish to retain a healthy scepticism of research proposals or projects that claim they are going to be methodologically innovative from the outset. How is it possible to know at the start of a project how we might need to respond, innovatively, to our research contexts? Moreover, how do we methodologically account for 'failure' in relation to our innovative research endeavours? What do we do if we fail? Almost by definition, innovation of any kind involves 'experimentation' and by extension experiments can go wrong, produce no results, the wrong results or contradictory results. So if we are going to support creativity and calls to innovation (and it is hard to imagine innovation without creativity) then we also have to be prepared to take and accept the risks associated with such pursuits. We should also remain realistic about what we can achieve in relation to enhancing good or excellent research practice and supporting continuous methodological development – the imperative to innovate can be disabling as well as enabling, and even come at the expense of well-founded research appropriately and sensitively carried out – existing and known methods used to good effect, with adaption and reflection where that makes sense.

In a narrative review of claims to innovation in published qualitative research, Wiles et al. (2011) concluded that, while there are considerable claims to innovation in the qualitative research field, these are often very difficult to substantiate. In their analysis, they found very little evidence to support claims for wholly new approaches, methods or research designs. In most cases where innovation was claimed, what was actually evident was some kind of adaptation of existing methods, or the transfer of methods to the social sciences from other disciplines, particularly the arts and humanities. Furthermore, Wiles et al. (2011) suggest there are considerable risks to over-claiming on innovation. Such claims can raise expectations that cannot be met, and can actually be a distraction – stifling the further nuanced development of well-established tried-and-tested methods and the ongoing need to engage with enduring methodological challenges. At the same time, a preoccupation with innovation can encourage an unhelpful view that established methods are passé and no longer appropriate for studying social worlds. Wiles and colleagues argue that 'different' does not always (or necessarily) equate to 'better'; innovation for innovation's sake, with no articulation or justification as to why a new approach is warranted does a disservice to the research community, and to the settings and participants with which we engage. Furthermore, it is also possible that overly focusing on method and methodological innovation can actually be a distraction from the very nature of the research 'problem'. Methodological development and innovation must have intent and purpose in relation to research problems to be explored and substantive research contexts to be understood. This is equally so for ethnography as for other social science research methods. Ethnography encompasses both method and methodology to foster exploration and understanding. Thus creativity, flexibility and adaptation in ethnography should always occur with an eye to the research problem – to increase our capacity to better explore, engage with and understand the research setting – on terms and in ways that make sense to our research participants.

THE FUTURE(S) OF ETHNOGRAPHY

The evidence-based policy and practice research movement in recent years has not been an easy space for ethnography to occupy (Hammersley, 2005; Leavy, 2014). The re-emergence of a scientism grounded in relatively narrow articulations of evidence-based epistemology – with a focus on systematic review, 'objective' data, causality and randomized controlled trials – sits uncomfortably with methodological and epistemological approaches which recognize and seek to understand multiple versions of complex realities; where 'epistemologies of critical race, queer, postcolonial, feminist and postmodern theories are rendered useless, relegated at best to the category of scholarship not science' (Denzin and Lincoln, 2011, p. 7). However, ethnography shows no sign of being in abatement. Ethnographic methods and approaches continue to be widely used across the social sciences, as well as in the humanities (Hjorth and Sharp, 2014). As a set of commitments and research practices, ethnography has endured for more than a century. The fact that there has been and continue to be a range of ways of 'doing' ethnography and of 'being' ethnographic is testimony to the capacity of ethnography to adapt and change, while remaining true to the conviction that the understanding of complex social worlds comes with participation, observation, interaction and experience. The disagreements, tensions and critiques within ethnography are also healthy indications of an ethnographic present and future; debates about what ethnography is and what it should be have always been part of the ethnographic landscape. In some ways ethnography of the future will be as of the past.

As has already been noted, ethnography, and qualitative research more generally, has undergone significant development and change over the last hundred years or more. Whether or not we are persuaded by the narrative of these changes as articulated by Denzin and Lincoln (2011), it is clear that ethnographic practice has not stood completely still, and that new perspectives, new approaches and new modes of representation have been brought to bear on how ethnographers go about their task. We might include here a range of ways of being ethnographic or of doing ethnography – the blurring of genres, alternative modes of representation and the opening up of new research spaces through debate and contestation (Coffey, 1999). Perhaps what is meant by ethnography has changed. As Denzin and Lincoln (2011) note, ethnography is no longer just about inquiry nor serves only as a record of experience, but has also developed as a form of moral and therapeutic practice.

Ethnography has been responsive to new methodological possibilities, and has and continues to extend its reach as a set of methods and research practices. For example, in recent years there has been an increasing engagement with arts-based practice, participatory ethnographic projects and cross-disciplinary and interdisciplinary work, as well as a reconfiguration of ethnography of and for the digital age. Potentially new ways of seeing or doing ethnography have been celebrated and abhorred in almost equal measure from within the ethnographic community; at one and the same time seen as a distraction and as the opening up of new ethnographic possibilities. Such tensions mark out ethnographic practice; ethnography can and does speak with many voices rather than always with one voice; the pasts, presents and futures of ethnography are many and diverse; the realities of contemporary ethnographic practice are multiple, complex and full of hope.

In many ways, contemporary ethnography has a complex landscape through which to navigate, situated within global changes, in a research environment that demands impactful, innovative and evidential research, while continuing to operate with an almost organic ebb and flow which supports really quite diverse research practices 'on the ground'. A focus on cutting edge innovation to ensure globally competitive and high-impact social science might be seen to be a little at odds with the nuanced and closely attended craft of ethnography. But this is not necessarily the case. Ethnographic research, used on its own or in tandem with other approaches, can generate data and analyses that can be used in impactful ways; responding to global challenges; telling powerful and empowering stories; informing and challenging policy. Furthermore, ethnography is an approach that can just as successfully operate on a global stage as in a hyper-local context. Indeed making connections between different levels of analysis, and across social and cultural settings, has been, is and is likely to continue to be a defining aspect of ethnographic research practice. Focusing on the craft of ethnography as we imagine the future of ethnographic practice is important. Craft implies a set of skills and tools with which to work, materials to shape and to understand, as well as choices of product to be crafted and 'made'.

So what of the imagined future of ethnography? There are a range of current developments in contemporary research methods which both draw on ethnographic approaches and have the capacity to shape future ethnographic practices. For example, within the social sciences more generally, we have seen an increased interest in mobilities and mobile methods, with a heightened sensitivity to developing approaches that seek to generate data through and in movement (Buscher et al., 2010). These include methods such as the 'go along', the walking tour and interviewing 'on the move', as well as the use of global positioning system (GPS) devices, that enable the geographical tracking of movement through space and over time. This methodological interest speaks to the broader development of social scientific work on mobilities as a field of study, seeking to understand social life in terms of flows and movement (Urry, 2007). Ethnography personifies the very idea of the mobile method, of course. Ethnography has always been conducted 'on the move'; the very nature of ethnographic fieldwork necessitates movement, fluidity and flow through settings. But the recent and wider theoretical and conceptual work on movement and mobility, together with technological advances that make it easier to capture moving data and data on the move, raise exciting possibilities for ethnography (see Fay, 2007; Ferguson, 2014). With scholarly interest in movement and mobility has also come an increased concern with place (Evans and Jones, 2011). Ethnographic methods are well situated to make further contributions here, able to capture movement but also to explore the lived understandings of geography and place. There are new possibilities opened up by ethnographic work that incorporates maps, mapping and map work. Of course, making maps and mapping terrains is a useful and well-used metaphor in and for ethnographic practice (Smith, 2005). Aside from mobility and the experience of movement, there are other, equally sensory, ways of doing and understanding social life. The recognition of and calls to multimodal ways of experiencing social life has led to an increased methodological interest in the development of methods that seek to capture different modes and modalities of experience (Dicks et al., 2005). This has included a heightened interest in visual methods, as noted elsewhere in this volume, but also ethnographic attention being paid to other sensory resources, such as sound and touch. Pink's work on sensory ethnography is particularly pertinent here, with her concern with the 'multisensoriality of experience, perception, knowing and practice' (2009, p. 1). Sensory ethnography, in this sense, has a dual meaning – 'a process of doing ethnography' that accounts for both the sensorial worlds of research participants and the ways in which the ethnographic craft is itself a multisensory experience. Pink's work enables a rethinking of ethnographic work to take better account of, and to afford recognition to, the senses of experience, perception, knowing and practice. She also locates sensory ethnography within the contemporary digital landscape. Enhanced use of digital and online platforms for undertaking research and representing research will continue to provide exciting new possibilities for ethnographic practice. It is difficult to predict what our digital and post-digital futures will be like, or how these will impact on how lives are lived and experienced, particularly given the rapid developments that have happened over the last quarter of a century. However, we can already see the ways in which technology of various kinds have impacted on how ethnography is practised. There are now a range of technological and digital opportunities for creativity with regard to ethnographic data generation, analysis, representation and communication. This includes a world of new settings to explore and understand, as well as a range of new and rapidly developing possibilities for advancing our capacity for real-time data linkage and data display. What might count as 'the ethnography' is also open to reinterpretation and shifting boundaries, with, for example, the possibilities of hypermedia ethnographic 'products', with the potential for reader interactivity and the capacity to trouble authorship and authority. Though, thus far, the opportunities for exploiting such technologies of ethnographic representation have not been widely adopted (Dicks et al., 2005; Pink, 2013).

Alongside these specific calls to ethnographic development, there have been more general developments in social research methods that have the potential to impact upon our ethnographic futures. The increased use and awareness of a wide range of social research methods, together with increased codification and methods training over recent decades, have brought some mixed messages for contemporary ethnography. For example, current discourses surrounding the preference for mixed methods approaches to social research potentially open up, as well as close down the possibilities for and of ethnographic research. The seeming imperative to operate with a methods 'tool box' – where we have all the approaches and techniques at our disposal to bring out and apply, depending on the 'question', is a persuasive and pragmatic argument. We select the best method or methods from a range in which we are equally skilled, depending on the research problem we are seeking to 'solve'. As pragmatic empiricists, we neither celebrate nor abhor particular methods, we treat them all equally, and use them in any combination that seems appropriate at the time. The danger of this view, however, is the potential loss of researchers' critical capacity to engage methodologically, epistemologically and ontologically, with methods divorced from their methodological, conceptual and disciplinary frameworks, poorly understood and often rather poorly executed. Mixed methods designs are often time poor and complex, and rarely have time built in for the prolonged and sustained engagement, that ethnographic methods demand, or at least are perceived to demand. As such, ethnographic methods often become reduced in such scenarios; an 'addition' that cannot hope to do justice to the capacity of ethnographic research to develop thick description and deep understanding through carefully nurtured field relations. There is a place, of course, for creative and integrated methodological approaches to research questions, problems, data collection and analysis. Ethnography can and does work well in and alongside other approaches. And indeed ethnography is, by definition, 'mixed methods' – combining a variety of strategies for gathering data in different media and modes, drawing in a range of strategies to data analysis and being open to representational diversity. But that is not what is usually meant by 'mixed methods' (see also Flick, 2018c). Often overly simplistically applied, mixed methods designs are more often than not taken to mean some simplistic and unreflexive kind of combination of qualitative and quantitative data. Within a more dynamic and expansive definition, more reflection is needed as to how ethnography can contribute effectively to mixed methods designs, enhanced by and not divorced from its methodological and epistemological frameworks and commitments.

Similarly, technology is both a friend and a potential enemy of the ethnographer. The large-scale adoption and endorsement of technological software and hardware 'to do' ethnographic research is also a potentially worrying trend. There are huge and exciting ethnographic possibilities opened up by contemporary technologies and virtual worlds. However, a taken-for-granted expectation that computer software packages are 'required' in order to undertake qualitative data analysis, or that all ethnographic and qualitative data must be gathered, managed and displayed in ways that suit technological fixes is, at best, unhelpful. Without critical reflection along the way, it is possible to imagine that an outcome of such a world view will be an ethnographic deficit of sorts. There is a danger that researchers 'practising' ethnography could lose their capacity to work with and beyond their data in meaningful ways, unable to think outside of the frameworks imposed by the technology. Equally, not all of social and cultural life is technologically mediated; nor can our understandings of digital lives be fully understood without recourse to broader theoretical and conceptual frameworks.

There has also been an increased trend for qualitative researchers more generally to wish to incorporate multiple data collection methods and modes of data within a single project, without necessarily thinking through the analytical affordances offered by and the problems of data integration. There are, of course, exciting possibilities for ethnography offered by integrating modes of data, and in practice ethnography has always worked at and in the spaces where different methods and data collide. For example, observation and conversation, the gathering of documents, artefacts and visual images, paying attention to speech patterns as well the embodied and practical accomplishment of everyday life. However, it is important that there is thought given to the ways in which projects might combine data and analysis in purposeful and meaningful ways. If a project proposes ethnographic participant observation *and* survey work, or collecting diaries *as well as* generating photographic essays, or creating soundscapes *alongside* ethnographic interviews, it is important to ask 'Why?' as well as 'Why not?'.

BACK TO THE FUTURE

The futures of ethnography will benefit from and continue to be influenced by ethnographic pasts and presents. The underlying principles and commitments of ethnography will stand it in good stead as it moves forward. When describing methodological developments or innovation, what is often at stake are advances or adaptations of 'method'. That is, developing research techniques and strategies to advance methods for data collection, data analysis or representation, rather than 'methodological' innovation. Of course, ethnography provides a range of methods for generating data and analyses which can be interrogated in order to develop our understandings of social life. But ethnographic research practice is also concerned with methodology; that is, with ways of thinking and theorizing about research.

Further engagement with the methodological possibilities and problems posed by ethnography, along with developments in and challenges to our methodological thinking, will ensure that ethnography continues to respond to changing times.

Ethnography is also well placed to contribute to realizing the potential of interdisciplinary working, both drawing together disciplines, as well working in the spaces between disciplines. Methodological development and innovative practice often takes place at the intersections and spaces between disciplines, and ethnography is at home here. Ethnography already has a wide and varied disciplinary reach (across the social sciences, but also across the arts, humanities and science subjects). There is, though, further work to be done. Formal research training and capacity-building work that speaks across and between disciplines is particularly hard to achieve. Developing more interdisciplinary ways of engaging in ethnographic practice could have significant affordances, providing a framework that serves to create spaces for creative dialogues between as well as within disciplines.

Finally, there is productive value in reclaiming ethnography as a 'slow method'; that is, an approach to research that 'takes time' as well as being 'in time'. Across the UK, the USA and elsewhere there has been the growth of what has come to be known as the 'slow food movement' (Andrews, 2008). This way of thinking about and preparing food is guided by a number of principles. Value is placed on preparing food with care, and the slow food movement is offered as an antidote to 'fast food'. Characteristics of the slow food movement include the sourcing and valuing of local, raw ingredients, ethical food production, global–local ties, the value of preparing food from scratch, and an appreciation of how different foods might work together and in combination. There is recognition of the skills involved in the thoughtful preparation and cooking of food, a renewed appreciation which savours the taste of food and the joys of eating together. From this perspective food has intrinsic and extrinsic value. These qualities provide a useful metaphor for reminding us of the value of what it is to approach social research with and through an ethnographic gaze. Ethnography appreciates and values global lives and local knowledges, and the co-production of data with care. It relies upon and is guided by reflexive and engaged ethical practice, along with a lived reality of experience. Social worlds and words are to be savoured; understanding is achieved slowly and in layers. While it is possible to undertake ethnography without years of fieldwork, ethnographic practice does take time. Good ethnographers also recognize and appreciate the ways in which different kinds of data and varieties of analytical strategy can complement and complicate each other. There are choices to be made in how we 'source' and put together our data, undertake our analysis and present the outcomes of our labours. 'Slow' can be a metaphor for other qualities of ethnography. Not only does ethnography take time, it also requires patience, skill, dialogue and reflexivity. It is through combining these ingredients that ethnography is practised and is made.

KEY POINTS

- The historization of ethnography has been described by Denzin and Lincoln (2011) as a series of 'moments', which capture the tensions, contradictions and hesitations that have shaped ethnographic practice over more than a century. While subject to some criticism, this framework has provided a reference point for considering ethnographic pasts, presents and futures.
- New global and hyper-local contexts provide new opportunities and challenges for ethnographic work. Communities are no longer bound or constrained by place, and new means of communication have transformed the ways in which global communities and local settings go about their daily practice.
- Technology has the potential to transform, as well as challenge, ethnographic research practice. New technologies provide new virtual research settings, and increasingly accessible ways of recording social life. Technology can aid data analysis and provide new representation platforms. It is important, however, to recognize that not all of social life is digitally mediated, and engaging with technology is not 'doing 'ethnography'.
- Innovation is part of the historical narrative of ethnography. Creativity, flexibility and adaptation are hallmarks of ethnography. There continue to be a range of ways of 'doing' ethnography and of 'being' ethnographic, while remaining true to the conviction that the understanding of complex social worlds comes with participation, observation, interaction and experience.
- Ethnography is well placed to engage in methodological discourses and developments, including in relation to interdisciplinary, mixed methods, mobility and place. There are also new opportunities for ethnographies that attend to multimodality and multisensory perceptions and experiences of social life.

FURTHER READING

Atkinson, P. (2015) *For Ethnography*. London: Sage
Burawoy, M., Blum, J.A., George, S., Gille, Z., Gowan, T., Haney, L., Klawiter, M., Lopez, S.H., O'Riain, S. and Thayer, A.M. (2000) *Global Ethnography: Forces, Connections and Imaginations in a Postmodern World*. Berkeley, CA: University of California Press.
Pink, S. (2015) *Doing Sensory Ethnography*, 2nd ed. London: Sage.

GLOSSARY

Autoethnography A qualitative approach to research and writing which draws on personal experience and self-reflection to understand broader cultural and social issues and processes.

CAQDAS Computer-aided qualitative data analysis, including using bespoke software packages.

Covert research Research undertaken where the identity and/or intentions of the researcher are not known to those being studied.

Cultural relativism The principle of understanding social structures, beliefs and practices from within a culture, and in reference to their own cultural frame of reference.

Epistemology The study and theory of knowledge, including methods, sources and limits of knowledge.

Ethnographic interview Qualitative research drawing on conversational strategies to elicit understandings and meanings.

Ethnomethodology Sociological analysis that seeks to understand the everyday and practical methods people use to make sense of their world.

Fieldwork Undertaking data collection in an existing social/cultural/organizational setting.

Gatekeeper A member of a potential research setting who controls and/or can give research access to the setting and its members.

Hypermedia The non-linear organization of information that can include text, sound, images, documents and hyperlinks.

Institutional ethnography A method of inquiry that considers how social relations are constructed through the ways in which social interaction takes place in the context of social institutions.

Key informant A participant in a research study who might act as a gatekeeper, or is able to provide particularly salient information or understandings.

Narrative analysis The formal analysis of stories and accounts of social experience.

Participant observation A method of qualitative data collection involving the researcher participating in and making observations of a social setting.

Postmodernism A movement within the arts, humanities and social sciences that rejects claims of one objective scientific method.

Reflexivity An awareness of the self within a social setting, and of the role of the self in constructing social action and understanding.

Symbolic interactionism Theory of social action drawing on the meanings people develop and draw upon in and through social interaction.

Theoretical sampling A sampling process and the selection of cases to develop and test emergent theories.

REFERENCES

Abu-Lughod, L. (1988) 'Fieldwork of a dutiful daughter', in S. Altorki and C.F. El-Solh (eds), *Arab Women in the Field*. Syracuse, NY: Syracuse University Press, pp. 139–61.

Abu-Lughod, L. (1990) 'Can there be a feminist ethnography?', *Women and Performance: A Journal of Feminist Theory*, 5 (1): 7–27.

Adam, B. (1990) *Time and Social Theory*. Oxford: Polity.

Adler, P.A. and Adler, P. (1994) 'Observational techniques', in N.K. Denzin and Y.S. Lincoln (eds), *Handbook of Qualitative Research*. Thousand Oaks, CA: Sage, pp. 377–92.

Alasuutari, P. (2004) 'The globalization of qualitative research', in C. Seale (ed.), *Qualitative Research Practice*. London: Sage.

Andrews, G. (2008) *The Slow Food Story: Politics and Pleasure*. McGill: Queen's University Press.

Angrosino, M. (1998) *Opportunity House: Ethnographic Stories of Mental Retardation*. Walnut Creek, CA: AltaMira Press.

Angrosino, M. (2007) *Doing Ethnographic and Observational Research*. London: Sage.

Atkinson, P. (1988) 'Ethnomethodology: a critical review', *Annual Review of Sociology*, 14: 441–65.

Atkinson, P. (1990) *The Ethnographic Imagination*. London: Routledge.

Atkinson, P. (1992) *Understanding Ethnographic Texts*. Newbury Park, CA: Sage.

Atkinson. P. (2015) *For Ethnography*. London: Sage

Atkinson, P. and Coffey, A. (1995) 'Realism and its discontents: on the crisis of representation in ethnographic texts', in B. Adam and S. Allan (eds), *Theorizing Culture*. London: UCL Press, pp. 41–57.

Atkinson, P. and Coffey, A. (2002) 'Revisiting the relationship between participant observation and interviewing', in J.F. Gubrium and J.A. Holstein (eds), *Handbook of Interview Research*. Thousand Oaks, CA: Sage, pp. 801–14

Atkinson, P. and Hammersley, M. (2007) *Ethnography: Principles in Practice*, 3rd ed. London: Routledge.

Atkinson, P., Coffey, A. and Delamont, S. (2003) *Key Themes in Qualitative Research*. Walnut Creek, CA: AltaMira Press.

Atkinson, P., Delamont, S. and Coffey, A. (2001) 'A debate about our canon', *Qualitative Research*, 1 (1): 5–22.

Bailey, C.A. (1996) *A Guide to Field Research*. Thousand Oaks, CA: Pine Forge Press.

Ball, M.S. and Smith, G.W.H. (2001) 'Technologies of realism? Ethnographic use of photography and film', in P. Atkinson, A. Coffey, S. Delamont, J. Lofland and L. Lofland (eds), *Handbook of Ethnography*. London: Sage, pp. 302–20.

Ball, S. (1981) *Beachside Comprehensive: A Case Study of Secondary Schooling*. Cambridge: Cambridge University Press.

Banks, M. (2018) *Using Visual Data in Qualitative Research* (Book 5 of *The SAGE Qualitative Research Kit*, 2nd ed.). London: Sage.

Banks, M. and Zeitlyn, D. (2015) *Visual Methods in Social Research*. London: Sage.

Banks, S.P. and Banks, A. (eds) (1998) *Fiction and Social Research: By Ice or Fire*. Walnut Creek, CA: Sage.

Barbour, R. (2018) *Doing Focus Groups* (Book 4 of *The SAGE Qualitative Research Kit*, 2nd ed.). London: Sage.

Becker, H.S. (1971) Footnote to M. Wax and R. Wax, 'Great tradition, little tradition and formal education', in M. Wax, S. Diamond and F.O. Gearing (eds), *Anthropological Perspectives on Education*. New York: Basic Books, pp. 3–27.

Becker, H.S. (1979) 'Preface' in J. Wagner (ed.), *Images of Information: Still Photography in the Social Sciences*. Beverly Hills, CA: Sage.

Becker, H.S. (1995) 'Visual sociology, documentary photography, and photojournalism: it's (almost) all a matter of context', *Visual Sociology*, 10 (1–2): 5–14.

Becker, H.S. (2007) *Writing for Social Scientists*, 2nd ed. Chicago: University of Chicago Press.

Becker, H.S. and Geer, B. (1957a) 'Participant observation and interviewing: a comparison', *Human Organization*, 16: 28–32.

Becker, H.S. and Geer, B. (1957b) 'Participant observation and interviewing: a rejoinder', *Human Organization*, 16: 39–40.

Behar, R. and Gordon, D.A. (eds) (1995) *Women Writing Culture*. Berkeley, CA: University of California Press.

Bengry-Howell, A. and Griffin, C. (2012) 'Negotiating access in ethnographic research with "hard to reach" young people: establishing common ground or a process of methodological grooming?', *International Journal of Social Research Methodology*, 15 (5): 403–16.

Berg, B.L. (2004) *Qualitative Research Methods for the Social Sciences*, 5th ed. Boston: Pearson

Berik, G. (1996) 'Understanding the gender system in rural Turkey: fieldwork dilemmas of conformity and intervention', in D.L. Wolf (ed.), *Feminist Dilemmas in Fieldwork*. Boulder, CO: Westview, pp. 56–71.

Beynon, J. (1987) 'Zombies in dressing gowns', in N.P. McKeganey and S. Cunningham-Burley (eds), *Enter the Sociologist*. Aldershot: Avebury, pp. 144–73.

Bloor, M. (2013) 'The rime of the globalised mariner: in six parts (with bonus tracks from a chorus of Greek shippers)', *Sociology*, 47 (1): 30–50.

Bluebond-Langer, M. (1980) *The Private Worlds of Dying Children*. Princeton, NJ: Princeton University Press.

Boellstorff, T., Nardi, B., Pearce C. and Taylor, T.L. (2012) *Ethnography and Virtual Worlds: A Handbook of Method*. Princeton: Princeton University Press.

Brewer, J.D. (2009) *Ethnography*. Buckingham: Open University Press.

Brinkmann, S. and Kvale, S. (2018) *Doing Interviews* (Book 2 of *The SAGE Qualitative Research Kit*, 2nd ed.). London: Sage.

Burawoy, M., Blum, J.A., George, S., Gille, Z., Gowan, T., Haney, L., Klawiter, M., Lopez, S.H., O'Riain, S. and Thayer, A.M. (2000). *Global Ethnography: Forces, Connections and Imaginations in a Postmodern World*. Berkeley, CA: University of California Press.

Burgess, R.G. (1983) *Experiencing Comprehensive Education*. London: Methuen.

Burgess, R.G. (1984) *In the Field*. London: Allen and Unwin.

Burgess, R.G. (1991) 'Sponsors, gatekeepers, members, and friends: access in educational settings', in W.B. Shaffir and R.A. Stebbins (eds), *Experiencing Fieldwork: An Inside View of Qualitative Research*, Newbury Park, CA: Sage, pp. 43–52.

Buscher, M., Urry, J. and Witchger, K. (eds) (2010) *Mobile Methods*. London: Routledge.

Cannon, S. (1992) 'Reflections on fieldwork in stressful situations', in R.G. Burgess (ed.), *Studies in Qualitative Methodology, Vol. 3: Learning about Fieldwork*. Greenwich, CT: JAI Press.

Carter, K. (1994) 'Prison officers and their survival strategies', in A. Coffey and P. Atkinson (eds), *Occupational Socialisation and Working Lives*. Avebury: Ashgate, pp. 41–57.

Charmaz, K. (2006) *Constructing Grounded Theory*. London: Sage.

Charmaz, K. and Mitchell, R.G. (2001) 'Grounded theory in ethnography', in P. Atkinson, A. Coffey, S. Delamont, J. Lofland and L. Lofland (eds), *Handbook of Ethnography*. London: Sage, pp. 160–73.

Clifford, J. and Marcus, G.E. (eds) (1986) *Writing Culture: The Poetics and Politics of Ethnography*. Berkeley, CA: University of California Press.

Clough, P. (1992) *The End(s) of Ethnography: From Realism to Social Criticism*. Newbury Park, CA: Sage.

Coffey, A. (1999) *The Ethnographic Self*. London: Sage.

Coffey, A. and Atkinson, P. (1996) *Making Sense of Qualitative Data*. Thousand Oaks, CA: Sage.

Comaroff, J. and Comaroff, J. (2003) 'Ethnography on an awkward scale: postcolonial anthropology and the violence of abstraction', *Ethnography*, 4 (2): 147–79.

Cortazzi, M. (1993) *Narrative Analysis*. Lewes: Falmer.

Crick, M. (1992) 'Ali and me: an essay in street-corner anthropology', in J. Okely and H. Callaway (eds), *Anthropology and Autobiography*. London: Routledge, pp. 175–92.

Czarniawska, B. (2004) *Narratives in Social Science Research*. London: Sage.

Davies, C.A. (2008) *Reflexive Ethnography*, 2nd ed. London and New York: Routledge.

Davies, R.M. (1994) 'Novices and experts: initial encounters in midwifery', in A. Coffey and P. Atkinson (eds), *Occupational Socialization and Working Lives*. Aldershot: Avebury, pp. 99–115.

Delamont, S. (1987) 'Clean baths and dirty women', in N.P. McKeganey and S. Cunningham-Burley (eds), *Enter the Sociologist*. Aldershot: Avebury, pp. 127–43.

Delamont, S. (2002) *Fieldwork in Educational Settings*, 2nd ed. London and New York: Routledge.

Denzin, N.K. and Lincoln, Y.S. (eds) (1994) *Handbook of Qualitative Research*. Thousand Oaks, CA: Sage.

Denzin, N.K. and Lincoln, Y.S. (eds) (2000) *Handbook of Qualitative Research*, 2nd ed. Thousand Oaks, CA: Sage.

Denzin, N.K. and Lincoln, Y.S. (2005) 'Introduction', in N.K. Denzin and Y.S. Lincoln (eds), *Handbook of Qualitative Research*, 3rd ed. Thousand Oaks, CA: Sage, pp. 1–32

Denzin, N.K. and Lincoln, Y.S. (2011) 'Introduction', in N.K. Denzin and Y.S. Lincoln (eds), *Handbook of Qualitative Research*, 4th ed. Thousand Oaks, CA: Sage, pp. 1–32

Dey, I. (1993) *Qualitative Data Analysis: A User Friendly Guide for Social Sciences*. London: Routledge.

Dicks, B., Mason, B., Coffey, A. and Atkinson, P. (2005) *Qualitative Research and Hypermedia*. London: Sage.

Elliott, J. (2005) *Using Narrative in Social Research*. London: Sage.

Ellis, C. (2004) *The Ethnographic I: A Methodological Novel about Autoethnography*. Walnut Creek, CA: AltaMira Press.

Ellis, C. and Bochner, A.P. (eds) (1996) *Composing Ethnography*. Walnut Creek, CA: AltaMira Press.

Ellis, C. and Bochner, A. (2006) 'Analysing analytical autoethnography: an autopsy', *Journal of Contemporary Ethnography*, 35 (4): 429–49.

Ellis, C., Adams, T.E. and Bochner, A.P. (2011) 'Autoethnography: an overview', *Forum: Qualitative Social Research*, 12 (1): Article 10.

Emerson, R.M., Fretz, R.I. and Shaw, L.L. (2011) *Writing Ethnographic Fieldnotes*, 2nd ed. Chicago: University of Chicago Press.

ESRC (2006) *ESRC Delivery Plan*. Swindon: Economic and Social Research Council.

Evans, J. and Jones, P. (2011) 'The walking interview: methodology, mobility and place', *Applied Geography*, 31: 849–58.

Farrell, S.A. (1992) 'Feminism and sociology', in S. Rosenberg Zalk and J. Gordon-Kelter (eds), *Revolutions in Knowledge: Feminism in the Social Sciences*. Boulder, CO: Westview, pp. 57–62.

Fay, M. (2007) 'Mobile subjects, mobile methods: doing virtual ethnography in a feminist online network', *Forum: Qualitative Social Research*, 8 (3): Article 14.

Ferguson, H. (2014) 'Researching social work practice close up: using ethnographic and mobile methods to understand encounters between social workers, children and families', *British Journal of Social Work*, 46 (1): 153–68.

Fetterman, D.M. (2009) *Ethnography: Step by Step*, 3rd ed. Thousand Oaks, CA: Sage.

Fine, G.A. (ed.) (1995) *A Second Chicago School? The Development of a Postwar American Sociology*. Chicago: University of Chicago Press.

Fine, G.A. and Manning, P. (2003) 'Erving Goffman', in G. Ritzer (ed.), *The Blackwell Companion to Major Contemporary Social Theorists*. Oxford: Blackwell.

Flick, U. (2014) 'Mapping the field', in U. Flick (ed.), *The SAGE Handbook of Qualitative Data Analysis*. London: Sage, pp. 3–18.

Flick, U. (2018a) *Designing Qualitative Research* (Book 1 of *The SAGE Qualitative Research Kit*, 2nd ed.). London: Sage.

Flick, U. (2018b) *Managing Quality in Qualitative Research* (Book 10 of *The SAGE Qualitative Research Kit*, 2nd ed.). London: Sage.

Flick, U. (2018c) *Doing Triangulation and Mixed Methods* (Book 9 of *The SAGE Qualitative Research Kit*, 2nd ed.). London: Sage.

Flick, U. (2018d) *Doing Grounded Theory* (Book 8 of *The SAGE Qualitative Research Kit*, 2nd ed.). London: Sage.

Fontana, A. and McGinnis, T.A. (2003) 'Ethnography since postmodernism', *Studies in Symbolic Interaction*, 26: 215–34.

Fordham, S. (1996) *Blacked Out: Dilemmas of Race, Identity and Success at Capital High*. Chicago: University of Chicago Press.

Fowler, D.D. and Hardesty, D.L. (eds) (1994) *Others Knowing Others: Perspectives on Ethnographic Careers*. Washington and London: Smithsonian Institution Press.

Fox, K.V. (1996) 'Silent voices: a subversive reading of child sexual abuse', in C. Ellis and A.P. Bochner (eds), *Composing Ethnography*. Walnut Creek, CA: AltaMira Press, pp. 330–56.

Gay y Blason, P. and Wardle, H. (2007) *How to Read Ethnography*. Abingdon, Oxon and New York: Routledge.

Geer, B. (1964) 'First days in the field', in P.E. Hammond (ed.), *Sociologists at Work*. New York: Basic Books, pp. 322–44

Geertz, C. (1973) *The Interpretation of Cultures*. New York: Basic Books.

Gibbs, G.R. (2014) 'Using software in qualitative analysis', in U. Flick (ed.), *The SAGE Handbook of Qualitative Data Analysis*. London: Sage, pp. 277–94

Gibbs. G. (2018) *Analyzing Qualitative Data* (Book 6 of *The SAGE Qualitative Research Kit*, 2nd ed.). London: Sage.

Glaser, B. (2001) *The Grounded Theory Perspective*. Mill Valley, CA: Sociology Press.

Glaser, B.G. and Strauss, A.L. (1967) *The Discovery of Grounded Theory*. Chicago: Aldine.

Gobo, G. (2008) *Doing Ethnography*. London: Sage

Goffman, E. (1959) *The Presentation of Self in Everyday Life*. New York: Doubleday.

Goffman, E. (1963) *Behavior in Public Places*. Glencoe, IL: Free Press.

Goffman, E. (1967) *Interaction Ritual*. Chicago: Aldine.

Goffman, E. (1969) *Strategic Interaction*. Philadelphia: University of Pennsylvania Press.

Gold, R.L. (1958) 'Roles in sociological fieldwork', *Social Forces*, 36: 217–23.

Goodall, H. (2000) *Writing the New Ethnography*. Walnut Creek, CA: AltaMira Press.

Gordon, T., Holland, J. and Lahelma, E. (2001) 'Ethnographic research in educational settings', in P. Atkinson, A. Coffey, S. Delamont, J. Lofland and L. Lofland (eds), *Handbook of Ethnography*. London: Sage, pp. 188–203.

Hall, T., Lashua, B. and Coffey, A. (2008) 'Sounds and the everyday in qualitative research', *Qualitative Inquiry*, 14 (6): 1019–40.

Hallett, R.E. and Barber, K. (2014) 'Ethnographic research in a cyber era', *Journal of Contemporary Ethnography*, 43 (3): 306–30.

Hammersley, M. (2005) 'Is the evidence-based practice movement doing more good than harm? Reflections on Iain Chalmers' case for research-based policy making and practice', *Evidence & Policy*, 1 (1): 85–100.

Hammersley, M. (2009) 'Can we re-use qualitative data via secondary analysis? Notes on some terminological and substantive issues', *Sociological Research Online*, 15 (1): 5.

Hammersley, M. and Atkinson, P. (2007) *Ethnography: Principles in Practice*, 3rd ed. Abingdon: Routledge

Harding, S. (1987) *Feminism and Methodology*. Bloomington and Indianapolis, IN: Indiana University Press.

Hecht, T. (2006) *After Life: An Ethnographic Novel*. Durham, NC: Duke University Press.

Hendry, J. (1992) 'The paradox of friendship in the field', in J. Okely and H. Callaway (eds), *Anthropology and Autobiography*. London: Routledge, pp. 163–74.

Hermann, A.K. (2016) 'Ethnographic journalism', *Journalism*, 17 (2): 260–78.

Heyl, B.S. (2001) 'Ethnographic interviewing', in P. Atkinson, A. Coffey, S. Delamont, J. Lofland and L. Lofland (eds), *Handbook of Ethnography*. London: Sage, pp. 369–83.

Hine, C. (2000) *Virtual Ethnography*. London: Sage.

Hjorth, L. and Sharp, K. (2014) 'The art of ethnography', *Visual Studies Journal*, 29 (2): 128–35.

Hockey, J. (1986) *Squaddies: Portrait of a Subculture*. Exeter: University of Exeter Press.

Hockey, J. (1996) 'Putting down smoke: emotion and engagement in participant observation', in K. Carter and S. Delamont (eds), *Qualitative Research: The Emotional Dimension*. Aldershot: Avebury, pp. 12–27.

Holman Jones, S. (2005) 'Autoethnography: making the personal political', in N.K. Denzin and Y.S. Lincoln (eds), *Handbook of Qualitative Research*, 3rd ed. Thousand Oaks, CA: Sage, pp. 763–91.

Horlick-Jones, T. (2011) 'Understanding fear of cancer recurrence in terms of damage to everyday health competence', *Sociology of Health and Illness*, 33 (6): 884–98.

Hunt, S. (1987) 'Take a deep breath in: an ethnography of a hospital labour ward', MSc Econ. Dissertation, University of Wales, Cardiff.

Hutheesing, O.K. (1993) 'Facework of a female elder in a Lisu field, Thailand', in D. Bell, P. Caplan and W.J. Karim (eds), *Gendered Fields*. London and New York: Routledge, pp. 93–102.

Jacobson, M. and Larsen, S.C. (2014) 'Ethnographic fiction for writing and research in cultural geography', *Journal of Cultural Geography*, 31 (2): 179–93.

Jennaway, M. (1990) 'Paradigms, postmodern epistemologies and paradox: the place of feminism in anthropology', *Anthropological Forum*, 6 (2): 167–89.

Junker, B. (1960) *Fieldwork*. Chicago: University of Chicago Press.

Kelle, U. (ed.) (1995) *Computer-Aided Qualitative Data Analysis: Theory, Methods and Practice*. London: Sage.

Kolker, A. (1996) 'Thrown overboard: the human costs of health care rationing', in C. Ellis and A.P. Bochner (eds), *Composing Ethnography*. Walnut Creek, CA: AltaMira Press, pp. 132–59.

Kozinets, R.V. (2009) *Netnography: Doing Ethnographic Research Online*. London: Sage.

Labov, W. (ed.) (1972) *Language in the Inner City*. Philadelphia: University of Philadelphia Press.

Labov, W. (1982) 'Speech actions and reactions in personal narratives', in D. Tannen (ed.), *Analysing Discourse*. Washington DC: Georgetown University Press, pp. 219–47.

Lahman, M.K. (2008) 'Dreams of my daughter: an ectopic pregnancy', *Qualitative Health Research*, 19 (2): 272–8.

Langellier, K. and Hall, D. (1989) 'Interviewing women: a phenomenological approach to feminist communication research', in K. Caiter and C. Spitzack (eds), *Doing Research on Women's Communication: Perspectives on Theory and Method*. Norwood, NJ: Ablex, pp. 193–200.

Lather, P. (1991) *Getting Smart: Feminist Research and Pedagogy with/in the Postmodern*. New York: Routledge.

Lather, P. (2001) 'Postmodernism, post-structuralism and post(critical) ethnography: of ruins, aporias and angels', in P. Atkinson, A. Coffey, S. Delamont, J. Lofland and L. Lofland (eds), *Handbook of Ethnography*. London: Sage, pp. 475–92

Leavy, P. (2014) *The Oxford Handbook of Qualitative Research*. Oxford: Oxford University Press.

LeCompte, M.D. and Schensul, J.J. (2010) *Designing and Conducting Ethnographic Research*, 2nd ed. Maryland: AltaMira Press.

Letherby, G. (2003) *Feminist Research in Theory and Practice*. Buckingham: Open University Press.

Lofland, J. (1976) *Doing Social Life: The Qualitative Analysis of Human Interaction in Natural Settings*. New York: Wiley.

Lofland, J. and Lofland, L.H. (1995) *Analyzing Social Settings*, 3rd ed. Belmont, CA: Wadsworth.

Lynch, M. and Woolgar, S. (eds) (1990) *Representation in Scientific Practice*. Cambridge, MA: MIT Press.

Lyon, D. (2001) *Surveillance Society: Monitoring Everyday Life*. Milton Keynes: Open University Press.

Malinowski, B. (1922) *Argonauts of the Western Pacific*. London: Routledge and Kegan Paul.

Malinowski, B. (1987 [1929]) *The Sexual Life of Savages in North-Western Melanesia*. Boston, MA: Beacon Press.

Marcus, J. (1992) *A World of Difference*. London: Zed.

Marechal, G. and Linstead, S. (2010) 'Metropoems: poetic method and ethnographic experience', *Qualitative Inquiry*, 16 (1): 66–77.

May, T. (2001) *Social Research*. Buckingham: Open University Press.

Mienczakowski, J.E. (1995) 'The theatre of ethnography', *Qualitative Inquiry*, 1: 360–75.

Mienczakowski, J.E. (1996) 'The ethnographic act: the construction of consensual theatre', in C. Ellis and A.P. Bochner (eds), *Composing Ethnography*. Walnut Creek, CA: AltaMira Press, pp. 244–64.

Mienczakowski, J. (1999) 'Ethnography in the hands of participants', in G. Walford and A. Massey (eds), *Studies in Educational Ethnography, Vol. 2: Explorations in Methodology*. Oxford: Oxford University Press/JAI.

Mienczakowski, J. (2001) 'Ethnodrama: performed research – limitations and potential', in P. Atkinson, A. Coffey, S. Delamont, J. Lofland and L. Lofland (eds), *Handbook of Ethnography*. London: Sage, pp. 468–76.

Miles, M.B. and Huberman, A.M. (1994) *Qualitative Data Analysis*, 2nd ed. Thousand Oaks, CA: Sage.

Mills, C.W. (2008) 'Sociological poetry', in J.H. Summers (ed.), *The Politics of Truth: Selected Writings of C. Wright Mills*. Oxford: Oxford University Press, pp. 33–5.

Minh-ha, T.T. (2000) 'Not you/like you: postcolonial women and the interlocking questions of identity and difference', in D. Brydon (ed.), *Postcolonialism*. London and New York: Routledge, pp. 1210–15.

Murchison, J. (2010) *Ethnography Essentials: Designing, Conducting and Presenting Your Research*. San Francisco, CA: Jossey Bass.

Narayan, K. (1999) 'Ethnography and fiction: where is the border?', *Anthropology and Humanism*, 24 (2): 134–47.

Nilan, P.M. (2002) 'Dangerous fieldwork re-examined: the question of researcher subject position', *Qualitative Research*, 2 (3): 363–86.

Okely, J. and Callaway, H. (eds) (1992) *Anthropology and Autobiography*. London: Routledge.

O'Reilly, K. (2008) *Key Concepts in Ethnography*. London: Sage.

Ottenberg, S. (1990) 'Thirty years of fieldnotes: changing relationships to the text', in R. Sanjek (ed.), *Fieldnotes: The Makings of Anthropology*. Ithaca, NY and London: Cornell University Press, pp. 139–60.

Paget, M.A. (1990) 'Performing the text', *Journal of Contemporary Ethnography*, 19: 136–55.

Paget, M.A. (1993) *A Complex Sorrow: Reflections on Cancer and an Abbreviated Life*. Philadelphia: Temple University Press.

Peirce, C.S. (1979) *Collected Papers*. Cambridge, MA: Belknap.

Pink, S. (2007) *Doing Visual Ethnography*. London: Sage.

Pink, S. (2009) *Doing Sensory Ethnography*. London: Sage.

Pink, S (2013) *Doing Visual Ethnography*, 3rd ed. London: Sage.

Pink, S. (2015) *Doing Sensory Ethnography*, 2nd ed. London: Sage.

Pithouse, A. (1987) *Social Work: The Organisation of an Invisible Trade*. Aldershot: Avebury.

Plummer, K. (2001) *Documents of Life 2*. London: Sage.

Pollard, A. (1985) *The Social World of the Primary School*. London: Holt, Rinehart and Winston.

Pollner, M. and Emerson, R.M. (2001) 'Ethnomethodology and ethnography', in P. Atkinson, A. Coffey, S. Delamont, J. Lofland and L. Lofland (eds), *Handbook of Ethnography*. London: Sage, pp. 18–35.

Ramazanoglu, C. and Holland, J. (2002) *Feminist Methodology*. London: Sage.

Rapley, T. (2018) *Doing Conversation, Discourse and Document Analysis* (Book 7 of *The SAGE Qualitative Research Kit*, 2nd ed.). London: Sage.

Reed-Danahay, D. (2001) 'Autobiography, intimacy and ethnography', in P. Atkinson, A. Coffey, S. Delamont, J. Lofland and L. Lofland (eds), *Handbook of Ethnography*. London: Sage, pp. 407–25.

Richardson, L. (1990) *Writing Strategies*. Newbury Park, CA: Sage.

Richardson, L. (2000) 'Writing: a method of inquiry', in N.K. Denzin and Y.S. Lincoln (eds), *Handbook of Qualitative Research*, Thousand Oaks, CA: Sage, pp. 923–48.

Richardson, L. and Lockridge, E. (2004) *Travels with Ernest: Crossing the Literary/Sociological Divide*. Walnut Creek, CA: AltaMira Press.

Riessman, C. (1993) *Narrative Analysis*. Newbury Park, CA: Sage.

Rock, P. (2001) 'Symbolic interactionism and ethnography', in P. Atkinson, A. Coffey, S. Delamont, J. Lofland and L. Lofland (eds), *Handbook of Ethnography*. London: Sage, pp. 26–38.

Rose, G. (2007) *Visual Methodologies*, 2nd ed. London: Sage.

Said, E. (1978) *Orientalism*. London: Routledge and Kegan Paul.

Saldaña, J. (2005) *Ethnodrama: An Anthology of Reality Theatre* (Crossroads in Qualitative Inquiry Series, Vol. 5). Walnut Creek, CA: AltaMira Press.

Sanjek, R. (1990) (ed.) *Fieldnotes: The Makings of Anthropology*. Ithaca, NY and London: Cornell University Press.

Schrock, R.D. (2013) 'The methodological imperatives of feminist ethnography', *Journal of Feminist Scholarship*, 5 (Fall).

Scourfield, J. (2003) *Gender and Child Protection*. London: Palgrave Macmillan.

Seidel, J. and Kelle, U. (1995) 'Different functions of coding in the analysis of textual data', in U. Kelle (ed.), *Computer-Aided Qualitative Data Analysis: Theory, Methods and Practice*. London: Sage, pp. 52–61.

Silver, C. and Lewins, A. (2014) *Using Software in Qualitative Research*, 2nd ed. London: Sage.

Silverman, D. (2011) *Interpreting Qualitative Data*, 4th ed. London: Sage.

Silverman, D. (2015) *Interpreting Qualitative Data*, 5th ed. London: Sage.

Small, M.L. (2009) 'On science and the logic of case selection in field-based research', *Ethnography*, 10 (1): 5–38.

Smith, D.E (2005) *Institutional Ethnography*. Lanham, MD: AltaMira.

Spencer, J. (2001) 'Ethnography after postmodernism', in P. Atkinson, A. Coffey, S. Delamont, J. Lofland and L. Lofland (eds), *Handbook of Ethnography*. London: Sage, pp. 443–52.

Spradley, J.P. (1979) *The Ethnographic Interview*. New York: Holt, Rinehart and Winston.

Stacey, J. (1988) 'Can there be a feminist ethnography?', *Women's Studies International Forum*, 11 (1): 21–7.

Stanczak, G.C. (2007) *Visual Research Methods*. Thousand Oaks, CA: Sage.

Stanley, L. (1990) *Feminist Praxis: Research, Theory and Epistemology in Feminist Sociology*. London: Routledge.

Stanley, L. (1999) 'Debating feminist theory: more questions than answers?', *Women's Studies Journal*, 51 (1): 87–106.

Stebbins, R.A. (1991) 'Do we ever leave the field? Notes on secondary fieldwork involvements', in W.B. Shaffir and R.A. Stebbins (eds), *Experiencing Fieldwork*. Newbury Park, CA: Sage, pp. 248–58.

Strauss, A.L. (1987) *Qualitative Analysis for Social Scientists*. Cambridge: Cambridge University Press.

Strauss, A.L. and Corbin, J. (1990) *Basics of Qualitative Research: Grounded Theory, Procedures and Techniques*. Newbury Park, CA: Sage.

ten Have, P. (2007) *Doing Conversational Analysis*. London: Sage.

Tesch, R. (1990) *Qualitative Research: Analysis Types and Software Tools*. London: Falmer.

Tewksbury, R. (2009) 'Qualitative versus quantitative methods: understanding why qualitative methods are superior for criminology and criminal justice', *Journal of Theoretical and Philosophical Criminology*, 1 (1): 38–58.

Thornberg, R. and Charmaz, K. (2014) 'Grounded theory and theoretical coding', in U. Flick (ed.), *The SAGE Handbook of Qualitative Data Analysis*. London: Sage, pp. 153–69.

Urquhart, C. (2012) *Grounded Theory for Qualitative Research*. London: Sage.

Urry, J. (2007) *Mobilities*. Cambridge: Polity Press.

Van Maanen, J. (1988) *Tales of the Field*. Chicago: University of Chicago Press.

Van Maanen, J. (2011) *Tales of the Field*, 2nd ed. Chicago: University of Chicago Press.

Walter, L. (1995) 'Feminist anthropology?', *Gender and Society*, 9 (3): 272–88.

Wiles, R., Crow, G. and Pain, H. (2011) 'Innovation in qualitative research methods: a narrative review', *Qualitative Methods*, 11 (5): 587–604.

Wolf, M. (1992) *A Thrice Told Tale: Feminism, Postmodernism and Ethnographic Responsibility*. Stanford, CA: Stanford University Press.

Woods, P. (1996) *Researching the Art of Teaching: Ethnography for Educational Use*. London: Routledge.

Woodward, K. (2015) *Psychosocial Studies: An Introduction*. Oxford: Routledge.

INDEX